CROQUET

PLAY·THE·GAME

CROQUET

Stephen Mulliner ·

Ward Lock Limited · London

Distributed by
STERLING PUBLISHING CO., INC.
387 Park Avenue South
New York, N. Y. 10016-8810

First published in Great Britain in 1989
by Ward Lock Limited, 8 Clifford Street
London W1X 1RB, an Egmont Company

Series editor Ian Morrison
Designed by Anita Ruddell

Illustrated by Peter Bull Art

Text set in Helvetica
by Hourds Typographica, Stafford, England
Printed and bound in Great Britain

British Library Cataloguing in Publication Data
Mulliner, Stephen
    Croquet, – (Play the game).
    1. Croquet, – Manuals
    I. Title   II. Series
    796.35'4

    ISBN 0-7063-6776-6

Acknowledgments

The author and publishers would like to
thank Peter Alvey for supplying the
photographs reproduced in this book.

Frontispiece: **Mark Avery playing in the
Inter-Counties Championship at Southwick.**

CONTENTS

FOREWORD

Association Croquet is possibly the best outdoor game ever invented. It tests physical, tactical and psychological skills equally and can be played on level terms by both sexes and almost all ages. The Croquet Association has been doing all it can to increase public awareness of the organized and competitive form of the popular garden game and has enjoyed an encouraging degree of success, particularly among young people. The National Schools Championship and the Junior Championship are now major calendar events and 17-year-old Chris Clarke from Blackburn hit the headlines when he won the 1988 President's Cup. Garden players have also proved to be a fruitful source of new recruits and the National Garden Croquet Classic has given hundreds of home enthusiasts their first taste of tournament croquet.

While there can be no doubt that the best way to learn Association Croquet is to join a croquet club and take advantage of its coaching and practice facilities, most novices are eager to supplement their new-found enthusiasm with an instructional manual. Until recently, there was an acute shortage of up-to-date croquet books and *Play the Game – Croquet* is a most welcome addition. It gives a succinct but thorough introduction to the technique and tactics of the modern game of Association Croquet and the detailed glossary in the Equipment and Terminology section will ensure that the reader is never at a loss to understand one of the game's many technical terms. The style of Ward Lock's excellent new series is particularly well suited to explaining the intricacies of croquet as it divides a potentially complicated body of knowledge into a small number of logical sections.

Stephen Mulliner is one of our most successful internationals and the 1988 British Open Champion. He is renowned for taking the battle to his opponent and seeking victory in the shortest possible time so it is no surprise to find that the main thrust of *Play the Game – Croquet* is directed at teaching a positive attitude to the game from the outset. Stephen firmly believes that a naturally aggressive player enjoys a substantial advantage over a more cautious opponent and, accordingly, whenever you step on to the court, your thoughts should be directed to establishing and playing a break if at all possible.

Play the Game – Croquet will be particularly useful to garden players. The correct way to play the full range of strokes is clearly explained and the tactical advice should allow the reader to spring some surprises on his or her regular opponents. By no means least, the book will provide a definite answer to those inevitable discussions about the rules.

On behalf of the Croquet Association, it gives me great pleasure to welcome *Play the Game – Croquet* and I am confident that it will encourage many who have played croquet only occasionally or not at all to give the splendid game of Association Croquet a try. You can be sure of a very friendly welcome at any croquet club and, if your interest is aroused, you too may join the ranks of those who have said 'I wish I had taken up Croquet much sooner!'

Martin Murray
Chairman, Croquet Association Council

HISTORY & DEVELOPMENT OF CROQUET

Association Croquet (pronounced to rhyme with 'okay') is the official form of one of the most popular garden games in the English-speaking world. It exists as a vigorous and well-organized minor sport in Great Britain and Ireland, Australia, Canada, New Zealand, South Africa and the United States and is growing steadily in Japan and several countries in Europe. The Croquet Association (invariably referred to by croquet players as 'the CA') is the governing body of the game in England and is responsible for the laws of the game and the organization of a calendar of over one hundred official championships, tournaments and weekend events. The tournament season lasts from April to early October and is punctuated by the three major domestic events, namely the Men's and Women's Championships held at Cheltenham in June, the Open Championship held at the Hurlingham Club in London in July and the President's Cup, the senior invitation event, held at Hurlingham in September. There are over 4,000 members of clubs affiliated to the CA and over one thousand active tournament competitors of all standards.

Croquet is a game for all ages and both sexes. Most of the best players are now aged under 40 and Mark Saurin, the 1988 Men's Champion, Debbie Cornelius, the 1988 Women's Champion and Spencer Ell Cup winner, Chris Clarke, the 1988 President's Cup winner, and Mark Avery, the 1987 Open Champion, were aged 17, 21, 17 and 22 respectively. More important still is the friendly atmosphere of croquet clubs and tournaments. The game's aristocratic heritage is more than sixty years in the past and modern players, although united by a love of the game, come from all walks of life. Croquet is simply one of the best outdoor games ever invented and well worth giving a try. It is also one of the cheapest to play and you can be sure of a warm welcome and helpful coaching from your local club for a modest sum. Contact the Croquet Association for details (see 'Useful Addresses').

Modern croquet developed from a game that probably made its first appearance in Ireland around 1830. Croquet arrived in England about twenty years later and soon became a popular recreation for the upper classes. The competitive merits of the game were also appreciated and a tournament held at Evesham in 1867 later became regarded as the first Open Championship. The All England Croquet Club was founded in 1868 and competitive croquet flourished until the emergence of lawn tennis in 1874. In 1877 the AECC changed its name to the All England Croquet and Lawn Tennis Club and in 1882 expelled croquet altogether because it was not making enough money. Competitive croquet went into hibernation until 1894 when a successful tournament was held at Maidstone. A new governing body, the United All England Croquet Association, was formed in 1896. In 1900 it shortened its name to the Croquet Association and retains that title today.

Croquet enjoyed a golden age from that revival to the outbreak of the First World War when it was once more a favourite occupation of those with time and money in abundance. Croquet parties were a common feature of the country house social scene and the game even received royal patronage. Fortunately, all this high living did not stultify the development of the competitive game and the emergence of three young Irishmen, Duff Mathews, Cyril Corbally and C.L. O'Callaghan, led to a revolution in technique and tactics. However, all this stopped abruptly in August 1914.

The end of the war brought croquet back to life but it had suffered considerably through the permanent closure of several clubs and the loss of many eminent players. The game recovered to an extent in the inter-war years and became a little less aristocratic in its appeal. The most significant development was the institution in 1925 of international contests between England and Australia for the MacRobertson Shield. This trophy, the Ashes of croquet, was donated by MacPherson Robertson, an Australian philanthropist interested in the game who had risen from rags to become a confectionery millionaire. New Zealand joined the Shield in 1930 and triangular contests are now held every four years. This period also marked the end of the old sequence game and the introduction of the lifting principle to give the outplayer a better chance.

The Second World War and the social changes that followed did even more damage to croquet than the First. Throughout the Fifties croquet seemed doomed to meander gently into oblivion as its adherents aged and new faces appeared only infrequently. The tournament game was dominated at this time by a triumvirate of croquet giants consisting of Patrick Cotter (b.1904), Humphrey Hicks (b.1904) and John Solomon (b.1933). So complete was their mastery that between them they won every President's Cup from 1947 to 1964 and every Open Championship but four between 1947 and 1968. Solomon was selected for the MacRobertson Shield side to tour New Zealand in 1950 aged only 17 and went on to become perhaps the finest player who has ever lived with a career spanning 25 years and 48 championship titles.

The outlook improved in the early Sixties when a group of undergraduates became attracted to the competitive merits of Association Croquet and began playing in tournaments. The word spread and the number of young players began to increase. Nigel Aspinall (b.1946) and Keith Wylie (b.1946) appeared in 1965 and demonstrated very quickly that they were of world-class standard. Aspinall won the 1966 Doubles Championship in partnership with John Simon, another young player, and both the Open Championship and the President's Cup in 1969. He has since won the Open and the Doubles eleven times each and the President's Cup eight times. Wylie was no less precocious and won the President's Cup in 1967 and the Open Championship in 1970 and 1971, beating Aspinall on each occasion. In the 1971 final he set a new

Nigel Aspinall playing at Hurlingham in 1982.

standard by completing the first delayed sextuple peel.

The CA has always encouraged the growth of Association Croquet but, until comparatively recently, a shortage of funds to devote to development and publicity hindered the formation of new clubs and the provision of adequate coaching for new recruits. Media coverage also left something to be desired with most newspapers and journalists being inclined to treat competitive croquet as a novelty or a subject fit for humour.

The situation has improved considerably since 1970. Aided by a Sports Council grant, the headquarters organization of the CA has become more efficient and development work has become much more effective. In 1985, a full-time National Development Officer was appointed and a National Coaching Scheme established. Croquet appears regularly on radio and television and the results of major tournaments are published in most of the quality newspapers. Individual membership of the CA has grown from under 600 in 1975 to over 1,600 today and the number of clubs has risen from 80 to almost 150.

The opportunities for international play have also increased. An annual international singles tournament has been held in California since 1986 and has provided players from Australia, New Zealand, Great Britain, Ireland and the United States with the opportunity to compete in an informal world singles championship. In 1988, the status of the USA as a major Association Croquet nation was confirmed by the inauguration of an annual Test Match against Great Britain & Ireland for the Solomon Trophy, the croquet equivalent of the Ryder Cup. The World Croquet Federation was also established in 1988 to provide the national governing bodies of croquet with an international forum and to hold official World Championships.

Association Croquet is a game with a venerable history which has developed into a lively and rewarding minor sport. Its appeal lies in the balance it strikes between the physical, tactical and psychological demands imposed by any sport on its competitors. You do not need to become a semi-professional to develop the physical skills of a croquet champion, considerable though they are, and if you can master the strategy and tactics of the game and put all this into practice under the most extreme competitive pressure, you too can look forward to competing one day at Hurlingham in the Open Championship or the President's Cup.

EQUIPMENT & TERMINOLOGY

Association Croquet is a game in which balls are struck by mallets on a court on which are placed hoops and a winning peg. Knowing your way around the court and the terms used in the game is essential if you are to understand the game properly. A word of warning: if you are familiar with 'garden croquet', do not necessarily expect that it bears much relation to Association Croquet!

The court

A full-sized croquet court or lawn (but not green) is 35yd (32m) long and 28yd (26m) wide. This is equivalent to two tennis courts and much larger than most people expect. Almost all outdoor courts are grass although experiments have been made with artificial surfaces such as those used for hockey. Indoor Croquet, using a carpet similar to those used for Indoor Bowls, was launched by the Croquet Association in 1987. The surface of a croquet court should be level and free from irregularities. It is particularly important that the boundaries are flat as delicate manoeuvres near the edges of the court can play an important part in a game. In tournaments the grass is cut to a height of only $\frac{3}{16}$in (5mm) or even $\frac{1}{8}$in (3mm) to provide a fast surface on which touch is of paramount importance.

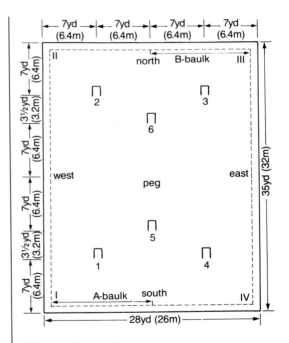

FIG. 1 *Court dimensions.*

Croquet can be played on smaller courts. The Croquet Association encourages the teaching of beginners on half-sized courts because it is much easier to learn break-play when the shots involved are shorter.

CROQUET

Boundaries

By a useful convention, the four boundaries of the court are named after the points of the compass, namely north, south, east and west. This has nothing to do with the actual orientation of the court. The south boundary is always the short (28yd/26m) boundary nearest hoop 1 (see Fig. 1) and the other boundaries are named relative to it. As you will see, this convention is very useful for describing the position of balls and the direction of shots.

Yard-line

This is an imaginary line running round the court exactly 1yd (90cm) in from the boundaries. It plays an important part in the game because whenever a ball leaves the court it has to be replaced exactly 1yd (90cm) in from where it went off. This distance is measured using the player's mallet or, in occasional critical instances, a yard-rule.

Baulk-lines

The baulk-lines are parts of the yard-line from which the balls can be played into the game. The A baulk-line, usually called 'A-baulk', is the western half of the south yard-line. 'B-baulk' is the eastern half of the north yard-line.

Winning peg

The winning peg, usually just called 'the peg', is placed in the centre of the court. It measures 18in (45cm) above the ground and is $1\frac{1}{2}$in (3.7cm) in diameter. It has a detachable part on top to which the clips (see below) can be attached.

Hoops

There are six hoops on the court. The four outer hoops are placed 7yd (6.4m) from their adjacent boundaries and the two inner ones

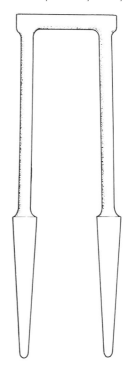

FIG. 2 *The championship hoop*

are placed 7yd (6.4m) north and south of the peg. A championship hoop is made of cast iron, weighs 6lb (2.7kg) and is rectangular in shape. Its uprights are $\frac{5}{8}$in (1.5cm) in diameter and are set so that the internal width of the hoop is $3\frac{3}{4}$in (9.5cm). The hoop is anchored firmly in the ground by substantial 9in (23cm) 'carrots'.

Order of the hoops

The six hoops form an obstacle course in which a ball is required to pass through each hoop twice on its way round, once on the outward circuit and once on the return circuit. Accordingly, each hoop has two names, one for each circuit. On the outward circuit the hoops are named hoop 1, hoop 2, hoop 3, hoop 4, hoop 5 and hoop 6 and are run in that order.

FIG. 3 *Order of the hoops*

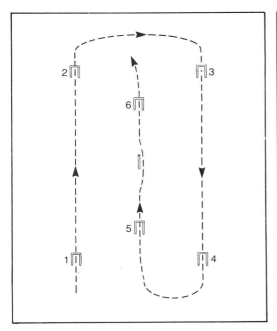 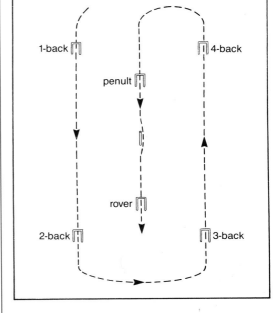

The return circuit involves running each hoop in the opposite direction and in a different order. The order of the return circuit is 1-back, 2-back, 3-back, 4-back, penultimate (usually called 'penult') and rover. You will see that hoop 1 is also 2-back and that hoop 5 is also rover. Hoop 1 has its crown painted blue to indicate the start of the course (and to provide an easy way of working out which is the south boundary) and rover has a red crown to indicate the end of the course.

The balls

There are four balls coloured blue, red, black and yellow. Each ball weighs $1lb +/- \frac{1}{4}oz$ $(454g +/- 7g)$ and in diameter measures $3\frac{5}{8}in +/- \frac{1}{32}in$ $(9cm +/- 0.8mm)$. This means that a hoop is only $\frac{1}{8}in$ (3mm) wider than a ball. A ball should rebound 30–45in (76–114cm) when dropped from 60in (152cm) onto a 2in (5cm) steel plate set in concrete. The balls comprising a set to be used in a match must have rebound heights that do not differ by more than 3in (7.6cm). The 'Eclipse' championship ball manufactured by John Jaques & Son Ltd is made of a compressed composition core with a plastic shell. Other manufacturers are experimenting successfully with plastics to produce a range of durable homogeneous balls.

Clips

There are four spring clips coloured to match the balls, and these are used to indicate the progress made by each ball round the court. This is done by placing the appropriate clip on the hoop that a ball has to go through next. If the ball is on the outward circuit, the clip is placed on the crown of the hoop. If it is on the return circuit, it is placed on an upright. If a ball has run all twelve hoops, the clip is placed on the peg.

Corners, corner flags and corner pegs

The four corners of the court are named after the nearest hoop and are referred to as either corners 1, 2, 3 and 4 or as first, second, third and fourth corners. Corner flags or posts standing 12in (30cm) above the ground are optional extras which are placed at the intersections of the boundaries. Corner pegs $\frac{5}{8}$in (1.5cm) in diameter and standing 3in (7.6cm) above the ground may be placed 1yd (90cm) from each corner flag along the adjacent boundary. The corners of the yard-line are called the corner spots.

Mallets

A mallet is the player's principal piece of personal equipment. Balls, hoops and the rest of the court equipment are provided by your croquet club. A mallet consists of two parts, a shaft and a head. Most shafts are made of wood, typically hickory or some form of ash, although metal and fibre-glass are becoming increasingly common. Mallet heads are predominantly wooden although durable plastic faces are becoming very popular. A few players have designed their own metal-headed mallets and all-plastic heads have a certain following. The laws of Association Croquet lay down no restriction concerning mallets save that the end-faces must not be metallic nor must the material of which they are made confer any playing advantage over wood. The aim here is to outlaw rubber-faced mallets and very hard materials which might damage the balls.

Most mallets weigh between 2lb 12oz–3lb 8oz (1.2–1.6kg), have shafts between 32–42in (81–106cm) long and heads between 6–12in (15–30cm) long. These dimensions reflect individual playing styles (see 'Technique') and physiques. You will not go far wrong to start with a mallet weighing 3lb (1.3kg) with a 36in (90cm) shaft and a 9in (23cm) head. Best of all is to try a range of mallets at a

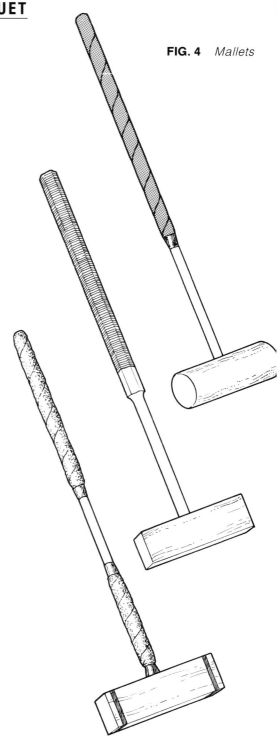

FIG. 4 *Mallets*

club before deciding which is best for you. Tournament mallets range in price from £40 to over £100. The good news is that the bottom-of-the-range mallets seem to be just as good at winning major events as the more expensive models. The author prefers a New Zealand model which can be imported for little more than £50.

Shoes

Flat-soled shoes are obligatory when playing to avoid damage to the court surface. Most tournament competitors choose from the wide range of tennis shoes now available. White bowling shoes are also popular. It is well worth spending enough to ensure comfort and a good fit. A tournament player could easily be asked to play five games in a day and you will soon find how tired your feet can get.

Clothing

Croquet is mercifully free from the detailed dress regulations typical of bowls. Predominantly white clothing is required for tournament play and some clubs expect it at weekends. The era of immaculately pressed flannels and club tie has passed and today's younger tournament players tend to dress in a manner equally suitable for tennis or squash.

Wet weather gear

Another of Association Croquet's hallmarks is its refusal to be halted by the uncertainties of a normal British summer. Rain does not stop play unless the court becomes waterlogged and so, if you plan to play in tournaments, you need a white waterproof jacket and trousers. Suitable garments can be obtained from bowls outfitters and from the Croquet Association.

CROQUET · TERMINOLOGY

Association Croquet uses a number of expressions which are peculiar to the game. We have already met a number in the Equipment section but there are several others you will need to know before you get the most out of the 'Guide to the Game'. The use of italic type in the explanations indicates another special term which is explained elsewhere in this section.

A-class players   Players with the lowest handicaps who tend to play under the laws of *advanced play*.

Address   A term for the stance taken up before a stroke is played.

Advanced play   The version of Association Croquet played by first-class players and at all major tournaments and championships. It is distinguished from *ordinary level play* by

special laws designed to give the *outplayer* a better chance.

Angle of split   The angle at which the balls diverge in a split croquet stroke.

Approach stroke   A croquet stroke in which the striker's ball is positioned in front of a hoop or close to a ball to prepare for a *rush*.

Backward ball   The ball of a side that has scored fewer hoops (see also *forward ball*).

Backward take-off   A form of hoop approach in which the *pilot ball* is on the *non-playing side* before the stroke is played.

Ball in hand   The term applied to a ball when the laws permit the *striker* to alter its position manually rather than by using his mallet directly or indirectly. The most common examples are (i) any ball when it leaves the court and has to be replaced on the *yard-line*, (ii) the *striker's ball* as soon as it comes to rest after making a *roquet* and must then be picked up and placed in contact with the *roqueted ball* and (iii) the striker's ball when the *striker* is entitled to a *lift*.

Ball in play   The term applied to a ball after it has been played into the game. It only ceases to be a ball in play when it is a *ball in hand* or at the end of the stroke in which it is *pegged out*.

Basic stroke   The single stroke to which the striker is entitled at the start of a turn. He can only extend his turn if he earns *bonus strokes* by either making a *roquet* or *running a hoop in order*.

Baulk-lines   Parts of the *yard-line* from which balls may be played into the game.

Bisque, half-bisque   A *bisque* is a free turn awarded to the weaker player in a *handicap* game. A *half-bisque* is a restricted turn in which no *point* may be scored.

Bonus strokes   If the *striker* makes a *roquet*, he earns two bonus strokes and can continue his turn. The first bonus stroke is a *croquet stroke*. The second is a *continuation stroke*. If the striker runs a *hoop in order*, he earns one bonus stroke, a continuation stroke.

Break, making a break   A break is a *turn* in which more than one *point* is scored. The standard form of break is the *4-ball break* in which the striker makes use of all the other three balls to help him conduct the *striker's ball* through the hoops. *3-ball breaks* and *2-ball breaks* can be played but are more difficult. While a break is in progress, the *striker* is said to be *making a break*.

Break down, to   To end a turn unintentionally by making a mistake.

Cannon   Cannons are strokes in which more than two balls are intentionally affected. They usually take the form of a *croquet stroke* in which the *striker's ball* makes a *roquet* and arise when the Laws deem a group of three *yard-line balls* to be in mutual contact. The striker places the striker's ball in contact with the roqueted ball for the croquet stroke in the usual way and then places the third ball in contact with the roqueted ball but not in contact with the striker's ball. When the croquet stroke is played, the striker's ball will hit the third ball immediately. Cannons involving four balls are also permitted.

Carrot   The part of a *hoop* sunk below the ground.

Centre style   The most popular style of play in which the mallet is swung between the legs rather than to the side of the body (see *side style*).

Condone, to   To notice that an *error* has occurred after the *limit of claims* has expired. The principal remedy no longer applies but a restricted remedy may be available.

Contact   In *advanced play*, if a player runs both 1-back and 4-back for one of his balls in the same turn and had not scored 1-back for his other ball before that turn began, his opponent is entitled to begin his next turn by lifting either of his balls and placing it in contact with any other ball and playing a croquet stroke.

Continuation stroke   A continuation stroke is either (i) the *bonus stroke* played after *running a hoop in order* or (ii) the second bonus stroke played after *making a roquet*. A continuation stroke is almost always a

Pat Hague playing at Bowdon in 1982.

single ball stroke which is usually used to make another roquet or to run a hoop in order. In rare instances, a continuation stroke can be a *two ball stroke* (see 'Rules Clinic').

Croquet stroke   The croquet stroke is the first bonus shot played after making a roquet. The striker 'takes croquet' by placing the *striker's ball* in contact with the *roqueted ball* and strikes the striker's ball so that both balls move. A wide range of croquet strokes can be played (see 'Technique') and it is this which enables *breaks* to be played and gives the game much of its tactical richness.

Croqueted ball   The term used to describe the *roqueted ball* after the *croquet stroke* has been played.

Cross-wire, to   To position both *enemy balls* on each side of the same hoop, usually the next hoop for one of the striker's balls.

Cut rush   A rush in which the *striker's ball* hits the *object ball* off-centre so that it is sent at an angle to the line joining the two balls before the stroke is played.

Distance ratio   The ratio of the distance travelled by the *croqueted ball* and that travelled by the *striker's ball* in a *croquet stroke*. It can vary from 10:1 in a *stop-shot* to 1:100 in a *take-off*.

Double tap   An example of a *fault* in which the mallet makes more than one audible sound when it strikes the *striker's ball*.

Double-banking   The term applied when two separate games are in progress on one court at the same time. One game uses the *first colours* and the other uses the *second colours*.

Double target; double   Two balls separated by one ball diameter. A double is equivalent to a single ball target at half the distance.

Doubles play   The version of the game when there are two players on each side. At the start of the game each side must nominate which player will play with which ball throughout the game. If a player strikes his partner's ball, a penalty is imposed.

Drive   A type of *croquet stroke* in which the degree of follow-through is neither exaggerated nor restricted. In a *straight-drive*, the *croqueted ball* will typically travel three to four times as far as the *striker's ball*.

Enemy ball   A ball of the opposing side. If you are playing red and yellow, then blue and black are the enemy balls.

Error   An event that requires the application of the Laws. Some errors result in the immediate end of the *striker's* turn. Others require replacement of the balls and cancellation of points scored but the striker is then allowed to continue.

Fault   An error made in striking the *striker's ball* (see 'Rules Clinic') which causes the turn to end immediately and the replacement of any ball affected by the stroke.

First colours   The traditional colours used in croquet, namely blue, red, black and yellow (see also *second colours*).

Forward ball   The ball of a side which has scored more hoops (see *backward ball*).

Forward rush   A *rush* obtained by running a hoop under control so that the *striker* can rush the *object ball* in the desired direction, usually towards the *next hoop*.

Free shot   A shot which is unlikely to give the opponent a break if it is missed.

Full roll   A type of *croquet stroke* in which the *striker's ball* and the *croqueted ball* travel approximately equal distances and in approximately the same direction.

Guard the boundary, to   To leave your balls near a boundary so that if the opponent shoots and misses, you can *roquet* his ball and use it to create a break. This may deter the opponent from shooting.

Half roll   A type of *croquet stroke* in which the *striker's ball* travels approximately half as far as the *croqueted ball* and in approximately the same direction.

Hammer stroke   A stroke played with the striker's back to the direction in which the *striker's ball* is to travel. It is normally used to make a *roquet* when a conventional stroke is prevented by the proximity of a hoop.

Hampered stroke   A stroke played with special care because of the proximity of a hoop, the peg or another ball. The *striker* commits a *fault* if he hits the *striker's ball* with the edge of the mallet-face in a hampered stroke.

Handicap   A number assigned to a player to indicate his ability. Handicaps range from − 2 (the best) to 18 (the weakest). Special doubles handicaps are sometimes awarded.

Handicap play   The version of the game in which the weaker player receives a number of free turns called *bisques* to give him a better chance.

Hit in, to   To successfully make a long *roquet*.

Hoop approach   A *croquet stroke* used to place the *striker's ball* in front of a *hoop in order* so that the *striker* can run the hoop in the *continuation stroke*.

Hoop in order   The next hoop that a ball has to run. Thus, once a ball has *run* or *scored* hoop 1, its *hoop in order* is hoop 2. If achieved, the *striker* earns one *bonus stroke*, a *continuation stroke*, and the right to *roquet* the other three balls again.

Hoop shot or stroke   A single ball stroke in which the *striker* attempts to send the *striker's ball* through its *hoop in order*.

Innings, to have the   To be the player who is more likely to earn *bonus strokes* in his next turn. If red and yellow are joined up close together and blue and black are each positioned over 20yd (18m) apart and over 20yd (18m) from red and yellow, the player of red and yellow has the *innings* no matter whose turn is next. If it is the turn of the player of blue and black, it is unlikely that he will *make a roquet* at that range and so he does not have the innings although he is the striker.

Inplayer   A name usually applied to the striker when he has the innings and is in the process of making a break.

Irish peel   A *croquet stroke* in which both the *croqueted ball* and the *striker's ball* are sent through the same *hoop in order*. See also *to peel*.

Jaws of a hoop   The space between the uprights of a hoop.

Jump shot   A stroke in which the *striker* hits down on the *striker's ball* in order to make it rise into the air and jump another ball, a hoop or even the peg. Jump strokes are also used to run very angled hoops.

Laying a break   The act of arranging the balls at the end of a *turn* so that the *striker* has a good chance of *picking up* and *making a break* at the start of his next turn.

Leave   The arrangement of balls at the end of a turn.

Lift   In certain circumstances (see 'Rules Clinic'), the laws entitle the *striker* to lift either of his balls at the start of a turn and play it from any point on either *baulk-line*. See also *progress lift* and *wiring lift*.

Limit of claims The period within which an error must be noticed if the full remedy given by the Laws is to apply. If an error is noticed after the end of the period, but before the end of the game, a restricted remedy may be available.

Line of centres The line joining the centres of the *striker's ball* and the *croqueted ball* before the *croquet stroke* is played. The croqueted ball should travel in the direction of the line of centres.

FIG. 5 *Running a hoop.*

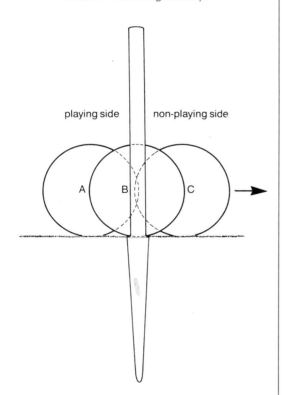

playing side   non-playing side

A: has not begun to run.
B: has begun to run, but has not completed the running.
C: has completed the running.

Next hoop The hoop that a particular ball has to run next in order. Usually employed in the context of the *striker's ball*.

Non-playing side The non-playing side of a hoop is the side to which a ball must pass in order to *run a hoop*.

Object ball The name given to a ball to be rushed before the stroke is played.

Opening The first four turns of a game. In *advanced play*, the opening is a tactical exchange in which both players attempt to obtain the *innings* without giving the other a good chance of a *break*.

Ordinary level play The standard form of Association Croquet as played in clubs. However, most tournament play nowadays is either *advanced play* or *handicap play*.

Outplayer The player who is not the *inplayer* or *striker*.

Partner ball The ball of a side that is not the *striker's ball* during a turn.

Pass roll A type of *croquet stroke* in which the *striker's ball* travels further than the *croqueted ball* and in approximately the same direction.

Peg out, to To cause a *rover ball* to strike the peg and thus complete its circuit and be removed from the game.

Peel, to To send a ball other than the *striker's ball* through its *hoop in order* by means of a *croquet stroke* or, occasionally, a *roquet*. See also *triple peel*.

Peelee The ball that is peeled or to be peeled.

Pick up The act of creating a *break*, usually from an unpromising position.

Pilot ball   The ball roqueted last before the *striker* attempts to *run a hoop*.

Pioneer ball   A ball sent to the next hoop but one for the *striker's ball*. If blue, the striker's ball, is for hoop 2 and, before making hoop 2, the *striker* sends red to hoop 3, red is a pioneer. If blue makes hoop 2, red will be the *pilot* for hoop 3.

Pivot ball   A ball positioned usually but not invariably near the middle of the court during a *4-ball break*. Its function is to shorten and thus make easier the *croquet strokes* used to place *pioneers* in the course of the break.

Plain hit   A *single ball stroke* in which the *striker* is neither attempting to make a *roquet* or *run a hoop*. It is usually played in the context of a *positional shot*.

Playing side   The playing side of a hoop is the side from which a ball enters the hoop in order to run it.

Positional shot   A *plain hit* in which the *striker's ball* is sent to a particular and tactically significant position on the court, often on the *yard-line* or in a *corner*.

Progress lift   A *lift* given in *advanced play* to the opponent of a player who has run 1-back or 4-back in his previous turn.

Push   A *fault* in which the mallet remains in contact with the *striker's ball* for too long.

Roquet   The *striker* is said to make a roquet when he strikes the *striker's ball* so that it travels across the court and hits a ball that he is entitled to roquet. At the start of a turn, the striker is entitled to roquet all the other three balls. If Andrew plays blue and blue hits black, one might say that 'Andrew roqueted black' or 'Andrew hit black' or 'Blue hit black'. 'Roquet', like 'croquet', is pronounced to rhyme with 'okay'.

Roqueted ball   The term used to describe a ball after it has been hit by the *striker's ball* and before the *croquet stroke* has been played. Once the stroke is played, the roqueted ball is called the *croqueted ball*.

Rover ball   A ball that has run all twelve hoops and can be *pegged out*.

Run a hoop, to   To send the *striker's ball* through a hoop. If the hoop is the *hoop in order* for the striker's ball, the *striker* earns a *bonus stroke*.

Rush   A short *roquet* in which the *roqueted ball* is sent to a specific position on the court, such as the *next hoop* for the *striker's ball* or close to a ball that the *striker* wishes to roquet next.

Rush-line   An imaginary line connecting the ball which is to be rushed and its destination and extended in both directions. It is desirable to play the approach stroke in which the *striker's ball* will take position for the *rush* from a position on the rush-line.

Scatter shot   A *continuation stroke* used to hit a ball which may not be roqueted in order to send it to a less dangerous position. Often used as a form of damage limitation when a bad *hoop approach* makes it impossible to *run the hoop* and continue the *turn*.

Score a point, to   The *striker* scores one point for every *hoop in order* and one point for causing each of his balls to hit the peg. As there are 12 hoops to be run by each ball, the winner will score a total of 26 points (12 hoop points and one peg point for each of two balls).

Second colours   The colours of the balls used in the second game played on the same court in *double-banking*, namely green and brown, pink and white.

Shoot, to   To attempt a long *roquet*.

Shot An attempt at a *roquet* of more than a few yards. A *long shot* is typically anything over 13yd (12m). A *lift shot* is a shot taken after the *striker* has exercised his right to *lift* the *striker's ball* at the start of the *turn*.

Side A game of croquet is contested between two sides each of which is responsible for two balls, either blue and black or red and yellow. In singles, each side consists of one player. In *doubles*, there are two players on each side and each player plays only one of the balls of a side during a game.

Single ball stroke A stroke in which the *striker's ball* does not start in contact with another ball.

Split A *croquet stroke* in which the mallet is swung at an angle to the line joining the centres of the *striker's ball* and the *croqueted ball* with the result that the striker's ball diverges from the path of the *croqueted ball*.

Stab roll A form of *hoop approach* in which the *striker* hits down on the *striker's ball* but restricts the follow-through.

Straight croquet stroke A croquet stroke in which the mallet is swung along the line joining the centres of the *striker's ball* and the *croqueted ball* with the result that the striker's ball travels in the same direction as the croqueted ball.

Stop-shot A type of *croquet stroke* in which the *striker* restricts the degree of follow-through in order to maximize the *distance ratio*. In a well-played *straight stop-shot* the *croqueted ball* can travel up to ten times as far as the *striker's ball*.

Striker The player in play at any given moment.

Striker's ball The ball which the *striker* chooses to play with at the start of a turn. During that turn he may not strike his *partner ball* with his mallet.

Take-off A type of *croquet stroke* in which the *croqueted ball* moves a very short distance.

Tice A ball sent to a position on a boundary close enough to an opponent ball to induce the opponent to *shoot* at it and, hopefully, far enough away to be missed. A tice is a standard feature of many opening strategies.

Triple peel The standard resource of the expert with which he can win a game played under *advanced play* in two turns. In his first *break*, he will take one of his balls round to 4-back and make a good *leave*. If his opponent misses the *lift shot*, the expert will make an all-round break for his *backward ball* in which he will peel the *forward ball* through its last three hoops (4-back, penult and rover) and *peg out* both balls to win the game.

Turn The basic unit of play which consists initially of only one stroke but can be extended by *bonus strokes* to a maximum of 91 strokes in level play. In the course of a game, the sides take alternate turns. The winning side is invariably the side that best develops its turns into breaks.

Uprights The vertical sections of a hoop. Also described as the *wires*.

Wire, a A term for a hoop *upright*.

Wire, to To interpose a hoop or the peg between an *opponent ball* and its likely target in the opponent's next *turn*, often the *striker's ball* or its *partner ball*. This is the croquet equivalent of the snooker.

EQUIPMENT · & · TERMINOLOGY

Wired A ball is said to be wired from another ball if the path of any part of the first ball to any part of the target ball is impeded by a hoop or the peg or if a hoop or the peg prevents a free swing of the mallet.

Wiring lift A *lift* given in all forms of play whenever the *striker* finds that one of his balls is *wired* from all three balls and was placed in its position by his opponent.

Yard-line The imaginary line running 1yd (90cm) inside the boundary to which balls sent off the court are returned.

Yard-line area The area between the *yard-line* and the boundary.

Yard-line ball A ball that is placed on the *yard-line* after going off the court or coming to rest in the *yard-line area*.

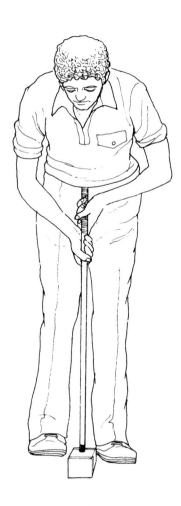

THE GAME – A GUIDE

Croquet is best understood as an obstacle race. The obstacles are the hoops and the object is to make both balls of your side pass through all the hoops in the correct order and then hit the winning peg before your opponent can do the same. This is simple enough. However, how you do it is a little more complicated and, even if you are familiar with garden croquet, you may need to read this section more than once before you understand the official game properly. In particular, you will find it helpful to refer to the 'Terminology' section whenever you meet one of croquet's technical terms, of which there are quite a few.

It helps to compare croquet to snooker and billiards. In all three games, the players take alternate turns which consist of just one shot or stroke unless bonus shots or strokes are earned. In snooker, the player attempts to pot a red and, if successful, is allowed to try and pot a colour, then another red, then a colour and so on. An expert like Steve Davis can clear the table in a break consisting of 36 consecutive pots, namely 15 reds, 15 colours and the 6 colours to finish with. A billiards player can also compile a break using a wider range of strokes, namely pots, in-offs and cannons. A billiards break can last much longer than a snooker break and, in the championships of sixty years ago, could contain hundreds of strokes. The principle of both games is the same – the inplayer continues until he voluntarily ends his turn, makes a mistake or wins the game. His opponent can do nothing directly to interfere and must sit patiently until the turn ends.

The same applies to croquet which has often been described as 'billiards on grass'. A croquet break consists of a range of strokes, namely roquets, croquet strokes and hoop shots. As in billiards, the opponent balls as well as the partner ball are used constructively to make the break easier to play instead of being banished to distant parts of the court. In an all-round break, an expert can play a maximum of 91 strokes in which the striker's ball will pass through 12 hoops and then hit the peg. Because there are two balls on each side, a game cannot be won with less than two breaks. In championship croquet, there are many games in which the winner completes the course for both his balls in just two turns. This is very different from the rather spasmodic progress typical of garden croquet where the players tend to make one hoop per turn and almost always in company with the partner ball.

A game of croquet consists of an opening, when the players fight for the innings, followed by attempts to pick up breaks and play them to successful conclusions. A good break will result in the striker's ball making as much progress as the striker wishes or thinks reasonable given the position of the balls followed by a good leave. This will give his opponent only long or dangerous shots to consider at the start of his turn. If the opponent misses or plays defensively, the original striker will hope to make further progress in his next turn. Ultimately, one of the players will reach a position in which he can peg out both of his balls and win the game. The initiative will usually pass from one player to another during the course of a game, especially if the players are below expert standard. Even in championship play, the outplayer is guaranteed a reasonably short shot and the innings will only infrequently remain with one of the players throughout the entire game. Nonetheless, to cater for this possibility, each match in the most important tournaments is decided by the best of three games.

The start

A game begins by the players tossing a coin to decide who has the right of choice. The winner then decides whether to take the choice of lead or the choice of balls. If he chooses to take the choice of balls his opponent automatically has the choice of lead and vice versa. The choice of lead allows a player to determine whether to play first or second. The choice of balls entitles a player to play with either the blue and black balls or the red and yellow balls. No other pairings are allowed.

Once the players have decided who will play first, the game gets under way by using the first four turns of the game to play each of the balls into court from any point on either baulk-line. As it is permissible, although difficult, to make roquets and score hoops before all balls are on court, the general principle of all openings is to avoid leaving a ball near either baulk-line or hoop

1. This explains why garden croquet players are often astonished when they see the start of an expert game for the first time. 'Why hasn't he gone for the first hoop?' they ask. The answer is that one hoop on its own means little and such an opening move would gain almost nothing and risk giving away a lot if the ball hit hoop 1 and stayed close to it.

The opening

Most players prefer to take choice of lead if they can and then to choose to play first or 'go in' but it is not uncommon in expert play to put your opponent in so that you play second. This ensures that you will have the first opportunity to play with all four balls on court and generally gives greater control over the type of opening. In level or advanced play, the most popular opening is the tice opening, although experts and adventurous players are often keen to use modern variants such as the corner 2 and corner 4 openings. Handicap play, where the weaker player is in receipt of one or more bisques, involves different opening considerations.

The main openings are described below in the context of a unisex match between Lucy and Andrew. Lucy won the toss and chose to go in. Andrew chose to play with blue and black and, accordingly, Lucy plays with red and yellow.

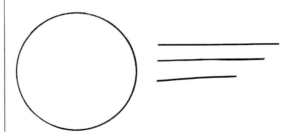

FIG. 6

KEY	R	Red
	Y	Yellow
	K	Black
	B	Blue
	R_0, K_0 etc.	Original positions of R and K
	R_1, K_1 etc.	Changed positions of R and K
	R_2, R_3 etc.	Later positions of R
	C	Ball to be croqueted
	S	Striker's ball
	T	Target ball
	●	Striker's ball
	O	Other ball

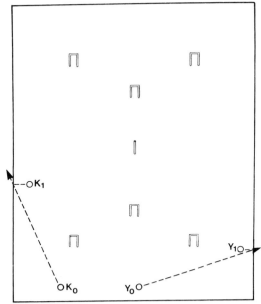

FIG. 7   *Turns 1 and 2.*

The tice opening

Turn 1   Lucy plays yellow from the east end of A-baulk to the east boundary 2 to 7yd (2–6m) north of corner 4. The exact distance is simply a matter of taste. Yellow is almost always hit hard enough to cross the boundary and has to be replaced on the yard-line opposite the exact point that it crossed the boundary itself. The choice of which ball to play is also a matter of taste. Lucy could have played red in this turn.

Turn 2   Andrew plays black from a point a few yards east of corner 1 to a point on the west boundary about 12yd (11m) north of corner 1. This is what is meant by 'laying a tice' as the 12yd (11m) shot from corner 1 is meant to entice Lucy to shoot at it with red in turn 3 in the hope that she will miss and so give Andrew the chance to join up safely with partner in turn 4. If black crosses the boundary, it is also replaced on the yard-line. As was the case with Lucy, Andrew could have played this turn with his other ball had he wanted to (Fig. 7).

Turn 3   Lucy now has a choice. She can either join up with partner on the east boundary or shoot at the tice with red. Three variations follow.

1   She shoots with red at black from corner 1 and hits. She now plays a croquet

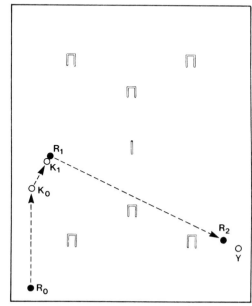

FIG. 8   *Turn 3: stroke 1 – Red hits Black.*
stroke 2 – take-off to Yellow.

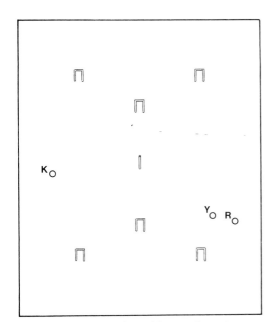

FIG. 9   *Turn 3: end position or 'leave'.*

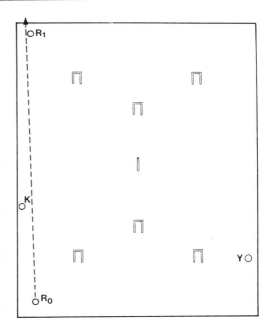

FIG. 10   *Turn 3: stroke 1 – missing.*

stroke in which black is sent a few yards further north and red travels across the court to yellow (Fig. 8). She now roquets yellow and lays a rush towards black further up the east boundary (Fig. 9). This is a strong position.

2   She shoots red at black but misses and red ends up in or near corner 2 (Fig. 10).

3   She refuses the tice and plays red from the end of A-baulk to the east boundary within a few yards of yellow (Fig. 11).

Turn 4   Andrew's play depends on the outcome of turn 3.

1   He shoots either (a) with blue at black from A-baulk so that blue will end up in corner 2 if it misses, or (b) at red or yellow from B-baulk near corner 3 so that blue will end up in corner 4 if it misses, or (c) at red or yellow from the east end of

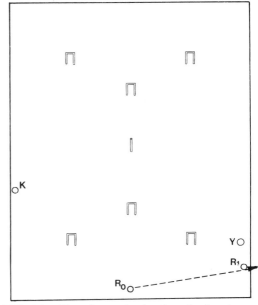

FIG. 11   *Turn 3: stroke 1 – tice declined.*

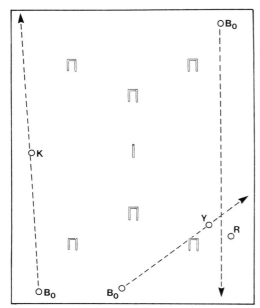

FIG. 12 *Turn 4: various options for stroke 1 after leave in Fig. 9.*

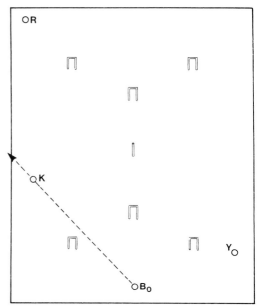

FIG. 13 *Turn 4: stroke 1 after position in Fig. 10.*

A-baulk, probably the shortest but most dangerous shot (Fig. 12).

2 He shoots with blue at black from the east end of A-baulk so that if blue misses, it will be replaced on the yard-line close to black (Fig. 13).

3 He shoots with blue at black from corner 1 so that blue will end up in corner 2 if it misses (Fig. 14).

The corner 2 opening

Turn 1 As in the tice opening.

Turn 2 Andrew plays black from the west end of B-baulk so that it crosses the west boundary 6in (15cm) south of the corner 2 corner spot. This will inhibit Lucy from shooting at black in turn 3 because if she misses narrowly, she will probably leave a double target for Andrew in turn 4.

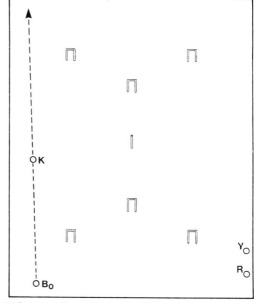

FIG. 14 *Turn 4: stroke 3.*

Turn 3   As in variation 3 of the tice opening.

Turn 4   Andrew shoots with blue at either red or yellow from the east end of A-baulk (Fig. 15).

The point of this opening is that Andrew hopes to hit in turn 4 and start a break. Making hoop 2 will be easier for him than for Lucy if he misses because the ball in corner 2 is his partner ball, not hers.

The corner 4 opening

Turn 1   As in the tice opening.

Turn 2   Andrew shoots with black at yellow. Two variations follow.

1   If he hits, he plays a croquet stroke which sends both black and yellow close to the peg. He uses the continuation stroke to leave a double target from either baulk (Fig. 16).

2   If he misses, black will be replaced on the yard-line close to yellow and may well leave a double target from the end of A-baulk.

Turn 3   Lucy's play depends on the outcome of turn 2.

1   She either (a) shoots with red at the double target knowing that she will give Andrew the innings and probably a break if she misses, or (b) plays red into either corner 2 or corner 4 hoping that Andrew will miss in turn 4 (Fig. 16).

2   She either (a) shoots with red at black and yellow from the end of A-baulk if they present a double target, or (b) plays red into corner 2 or a few yards south of corner 2.

Turn 4   Andrew's play depends on the outcome of turn 3.

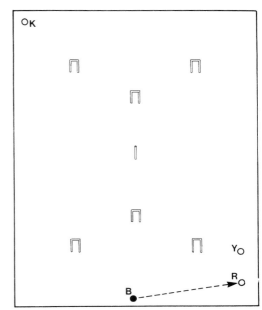

FIG. 15   *Turn 4: Blue shoots at Red.*

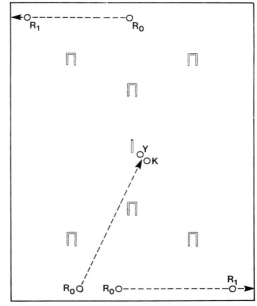

FIG. 16   *Red has a double target from either baulk.*

**Paul Skinley of New Zealand playing in the first
Test Match against the United Kingdom at
Cheltenham in 1986.**

1 If Lucy has missed with red (sub-variation (a)), red will have finished in or very close to one of the baulks and Andrew will make an easy roquet with blue on red and hope to start a break. If Lucy played red into corner 2 or 4 (sub-variation (b)), Andrew will shoot with blue at the double target of black and yellow, probably from near corner 1 so that if he misses, blue will finish as far away from hoop 1 as possible.

2 If Lucy hit on turn 3, Andrew will probably be in much the same position as if she hit on turn 3 of the tice opening and will play as in variation **1** in turn 4 of that opening. If she missed or played into corner 2, Andrew will shoot with blue at the balls on the east boundary as in turn 4 of the corner 2 opening.

The idea of this opening is to force the issue and to prevent the opening becoming a tactical battle preferred by experts whose tactics are better than their shooting. For this reason, it is often used by novice players.

The 4-ball break

We will rejoin Lucy and Andrew after their game has been in progress for a while to see a turn in which a 4-ball break is played. This is a level game so no bisques (used in handicap play) or progress lifts (used in advanced play) will be involved. Refer back to the 'Terminology' section if you are unsure about the meaning of a term. Andrew has reached the peg with blue and is still for hoop 1 with black. He has left his balls near corner 4, red near hoop 1 and yellow near hoop 2 and it is now Lucy's turn. She is for the peg with red and 3-back with yellow and is therefore in the lead in terms of points scored. However, she knows that Andrew has the innings and is capable of finishing the game in his next turn so her lead may turn out to be strictly temporary.

Lucy has a range of choices but finally chooses to take the 16yd (15m) shot with red

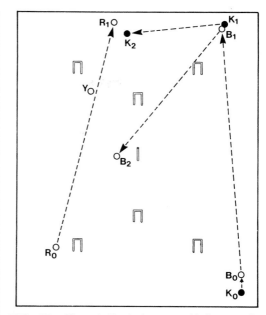

FIG. 17 *Turn 1: Red shoots at Yellow and misses.*
Turn 2: stroke 1 – Black rushes Blue to the north boundary. stroke 2 – croquet stroke placing Blue near the peg and Black near Red.

at yellow, an aggressive but justifiable decision given that she strongly suspects that Andrew will be able to establish a break even if she corners (see 'Technique'). However, she misses and Andrew steps onto the court with the balls as shown (Fig. 17).

Andrew obviously chooses to play with black, the backward ball, as blue, the forward ball, has no more hoops to make. He uses the basic stroke to which he is entitled to make a roquet on blue with black and thus earns two bonus strokes, a croquet stroke followed by a continuation stroke. In fact, the roquet on blue is more correctly described as a rush because Andrew hits black with enough force to send blue to the north boundary about 8yd (7m) east of red.

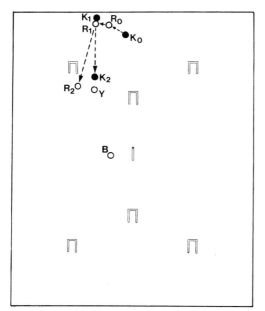

FIG. 18 *Turn 2: stroke 3 – Black roquets Red.
stroke 4 – croquet stroke placing Red near hoop 2 and Black near Yellow.*

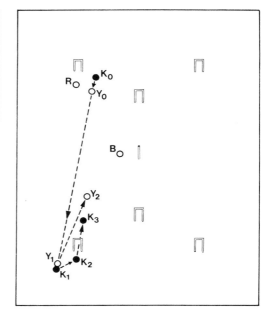

FIG. 19 *Stroke 5 – Black rushes Yellow south of hoop 1.
Stroke 6 – hoop approach placing Yellow beyond the hoop and Black in position to run the hoop.
Stroke 7 – Black runs the hoop.*

In the croquet stroke, Andrew plays a stop-shot which sends blue about 3yd (3m) west of the peg while black stops close to red. Andrew uses the continuation stroke to make another roquet, this time on red, and so earns another two bonus strokes (Fig. 18).

The bonus strokes again consist of a croquet stroke followed by a continuation stroke. This time the croquet stroke is a gentle roll which sends red about 2ft (60cm) south of hoop 2 and black about 2ft (60cm) north of yellow so that Andrew has a straight rush on yellow to hoop 1 (Fig. 18). In the continuation stroke, Andrew rushes yellow with black all the way down to hoop 1 and, for the third time, earns two bonus strokes.

Andrew's rush was a good one and yellow comes to rest 4ft (120cm) south and slightly west of hoop 1. His first bonus stroke, the

croquet stroke and the third of the turn so far, is a stop-shot which sends yellow 4yd (4m) north of hoop 1 while black moves only 3ft (90cm) to a position 1ft (30cm) south of the hoop, in good position to run it. The second bonus stroke, the continuation stroke, is not used to make a roquet on this occasion. Instead, Andrew hits black gently through the hoop so that it comes to rest just short of yellow (Fig. 19).

Running the hoop earns Andrew only one bonus stroke, a continuation stroke, but he also earns the right to roquet each of the other three balls again and thus earn further bonus strokes.

Andrew uses this continuation stroke to rush yellow about 4yd (4m) short of blue. Making a roquet on yellow earns the usual two bonus strokes and the croquet stroke is used to stop-shot yellow to hoop 3 while

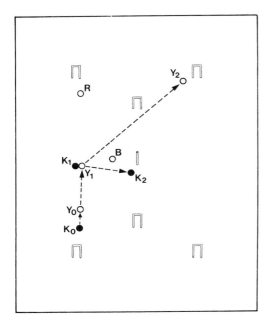

FIG. 20 *Stroke 8 – Black rushes Yellow towards Blue.*
Stroke 9 – croquet stroke sending Yellow to hoop 3 and Black near to Blue.

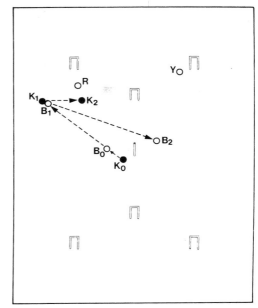

FIG. 21 *Stroke 10 – Black rushes Blue past Red. Stroke 11 – croquet stroke sending Blue back to the peg and Black near Red.*

black stops close to blue (Fig. 20). The continuation stroke is used to rush blue just beyond red at hoop 2.

This roquet also earns two bonus strokes. The croquet stroke is used to stop-shot blue back to the middle of the court while black ends just past red (Fig. 21). The continuation stroke is used to make a gentle roquet on red which entitles Andrew to play a tiny croquet stroke, a stop-shot which sends red just past the east side of hoop 2 while black stops a few inches in front of the hoop. The second bonus stroke resulting from the roquet on red is the continuation stroke which Andrew uses to send black a couple of feet through hoop 2 (Fig. 22).

The next few strokes can be described more briefly as the pattern should be becoming clearer. Having run hoop 2 and earned one continuation stroke, Andrew

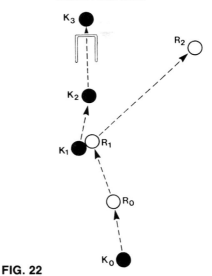

FIG. 22

Stroke 12 – Black roquets Red towards hoop 2.
Stroke 13 – hoop approach.
Stroke 14 – Black runs the hoop.

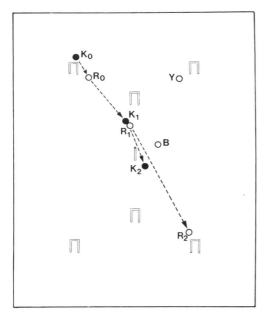

FIG. 23   *Stroke 15 – Black rushes Red towards Blue.*
Stroke 16 – croquet stroke sending Red to hoop 4 and Black near Blue.

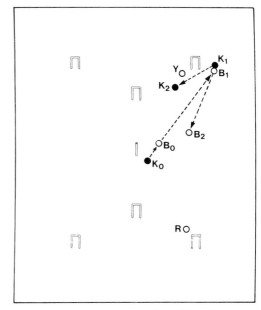

FIG. 24   *Stroke 17 – Black rushes Blue past Yellow. Stroke 18 – croquet stroke sending Blue back towards peg and Black near Yellow.*

roquets red and plays a croquet stroke which sends red to hoop 4 while black goes near blue (Fig. 23), roquets blue back beyond yellow at hoop 3 and stop-shots blue back to near the peg while black stays close to yellow (Fig. 24), roquets yellow in front of hoop 3 and stop-shots yellow a few feet south of hoop 3 while black stops in front of the hoop. With the continuation stroke, Andrew runs hoop 3 (Fig. 25).

A number of points should now be clear. First, there is a repeated seven-stroke pattern between each hoop consisting of roquet, croquet stroke, roquet, croquet stroke, roquet, croquet stroke and hoop stroke. Second, all the balls are used as stepping-stones to help black go from hoop to hoop. Check the meanings of the terms *pilot*, *pivot* and *pioneer* in the 'Terminology' section. Before Andrew ran hoop 1, yellow was the pilot, yellow became a pioneer for hoop 3 and blue remained the pivot. After

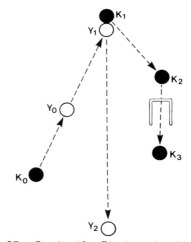

FIG. 25   *Stroke 19 – Black rushes Yellow north of hoop 3.*
Stroke 20 – hoop approach sending Yellow beyond the hoop and Black in position to run.
Stroke 21 – Black runs the hoop.

hoop 2, yellow once more became the pilot — for hoop 3 — while red became the hoop 4 pioneer. Blue remained the pivot. If you understand the stepping-stone sequence and these rather appropriate terms for the balls used in a 4-ball break, you have mastered much of the theory of break-play.

The rest of the break can be summarized quite quickly. Andrew makes hoops 4, 6, 2-back, 4-back and rover (the even-numbered hoops) off red (i.e. using red as the pilot in each case) and hoops 5, 1-back, 3-back and penult off yellow. Blue remains the pivot throughout the break, being rushed towards the next hoop to be made and then croqueted back towards the middle of the court on each occasion. After running rover, Andrew roquets red for the last time, uses the croquet stroke to get a rush on yellow towards blue which is waiting by the peg and, having roqueted and croqueted yellow, rushes blue to within a few inches of the peg. He lines up the croquet stroke with the centre of the peg and plays a firm straight stop-shot which makes blue hit the peg. Blue is then removed and, with the continuation stroke, Andrew hits black onto the peg and wins the game.

2- and 3-ball breaks

It is quite possible to play a break with pilots and pioneers but no pivot. This is called a 3-ball break and is more difficult than a 4-ball break because the absence of a pivot increases the size of the croquet strokes required to place the pioneers and thus the likelihood that they will be poorly positioned. It is possible to mitigate this difficulty to an extent by obtaining a forward rush after each hoop so that every big croquet stroke is a straight stop-shot. This is the type of croquet stroke in which the striker's ball moves least relative to the croqueted ball and is thus the most accurate.

A 2-ball break is much more difficult than a 3-ball break because there is no pioneer as well as no pivot. The success of the break relies upon the striker obtaining good forward rushes after every hoop towards the next hoop and, when he fails to achieve this, playing accurate long hoop approaches and running some difficult hoops. The best players are capable of playing an all-round 2-ball break on an easy-paced lawn and it is a splendid form of practice to which the novice player can look forward.

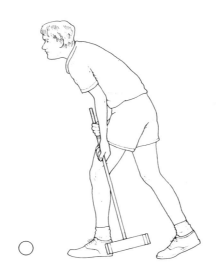

RULES
CLINIC

Can you run hoops and make roquets before all four balls are in play?

Yes.

Is there a sequence rule?

No. It was abolished in 1920. At the start of a turn the striker can choose to play with either of his balls. He must stick to his choice throughout that turn. He can play with the same ball for several turns in succession if he wants to.

Can you put a foot on the striker's ball when playing a croquet stroke?

No. This was abolished in the last century. It is now a fault and your turn would end.

What happens if you run a hoop and make a roquet in the same stroke?

You take croquet immediately. The roquet is deemed to have been made.

What happens if you run two hoops in the same stroke?

You get only one bonus stroke.

When does a ball complete the running of a hoop?

When the back of the ball cannot be touched by a straight edge placed against the playing side of the hoop (Fig. 5).

What happens if the striker runs a hoop but, before completing the running, hits a ball that was clear of the hoop before the stroke?

The hoop is deemed to be scored before the roquet is made. Note that the striker's ball must have completed the running of the hoop when it comes to rest. If it does not, the hoop will not be scored and the turn will end unless the striker was entitled to roquet the ball in question even without running the hoop.

What happens if the striker's ball hits two balls which it is entitled to roquet?

The roquet is made on the first ball to be hit. If both were hit simultaneously the striker can choose.

What happens if a rover ball hits the peg and a ball which it is entitled to roquet simultaneously?

The striker can choose whether the roquet is made or the peg point is scored.

What happens if the striker's ball runs a hoop in a croquet stroke and then hits the croqueted ball again?

The roquet is deemed not to be made unless the balls end up in contact.

What happens if the balls do end up in contact after a croquet stroke but the striker's ball did not run a hoop in that stroke?

A continuation stroke is played as usual. However, the stroke is a two-ball stroke and so it may well be rather difficult to make a roquet or run a hoop.

What happens if I find one of my balls in contact with another at the start of a turn?

If you choose to play with it you must start with a croquet stroke. The same applies if you run a hoop to the boundary and replace the striker's ball on the yard-line. If it has to be placed in contact with another ball, you must play a croquet stroke immediately.

Is there any penalty if a ball is sent over the boundary in a single ball stroke?

No. In a hoop shot, the striker's ball is replaced on the yard-line and the turn continues. If you make a roquet and the roqueted ball goes off, it is replaced on the yard-line and the croquet stroke is played from there. If the striker's ball goes off, it becomes a ball in hand anyway and is placed for the croquet stroke in the usual way.

Is there a penalty if a ball is sent off the court in a croquet stroke?

Yes. If the croqueted ball is sent off, the turn ends immediately. If the striker's ball is sent off, the same applies unless it either ran a hoop in order or made a roquet in the course of the stroke before going off. Note that there are no exceptions for the croqueted ball, not even if it it is peeled through its next hoop before going off.

When is a ball considered off the court?

A ball leaves the court when any part of it would touch an imaginary wall raised vertically from the inner edge of the boundary.

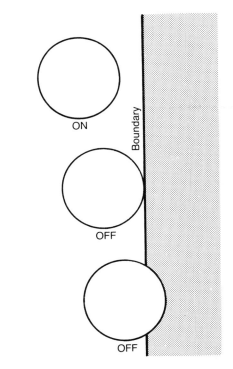

FIG. 26   *Judging when a ball is off the court.*

What happens if a ball goes off and then rolls back into the court?

It is still considered to be off the court.

What is the penalty for playing when not entitled to do so?

This usually happens when the striker carries on playing after running a wrong hoop. All play after the striker ceases to be entitled to play is cancelled and the balls are replaced.

What is the penalty for playing a wrong ball?

The striker's turn ends. All play after the wrong ball is struck is cancelled and the balls are replaced in the positions they occupied before the wrong ball was struck.

What happens if the striker takes croquet from the wrong ball?

The offender's turn does not end but his opponent has the choice of demanding a replay using the correct ball or permitting the croquet stroke to stand with the wrong ball interchanged with the correct ball.

What happens if the striker fails to take croquet when he should or takes croquet before making a roquet?

In each case, the balls are replaced and the striker continues his turn correctly.

What happens if a ball is wrongly pegged out or, having been correctly pegged out, is not removed from the court?

The balls are replaced in the positions they occupied before the error was committed and the player then in play continues without penalty.

What happens to the score when balls have to be replaced because an error is discovered?

The general rule is that any hoops scored after an error do not count if the balls have to be replaced. There are some exceptions to this if the error is discovered at a later stage but, in practice, errors are usually discovered at once or not at all. However, if you want to play in tournaments, you will need to buy a copy of the official Laws and study it carefully.

What is a fault and what happens if a fault is committed?

A fault is an error of execution in playing a stroke. The penalty is the immediate end to the turn and the replacement of the balls and the cancellation of any hoop scored in the stroke. The Laws list sixteen separate faults but the most important ones are:

  (a) touching the head of the mallet with your hand;
  (b) failing to hit the striker's ball cleanly (this covers pushing, double-tapping and hitting the ball with the edge of the face in a hampered stroke);
  (c) crushing or squeezing the striker's ball against a hoop or the peg;
  (d) touching any ball with your clothes or any ball other than the striker's ball with the mallet; and
  (e) failing to move or shake the croqueted ball in a croquet stroke.

Note that these only apply during the striking period, namely from the beginning of the backswing to when you quit your stance under control. If you jump up in the air to avoid the striker's ball hitting your foot and land on another ball, bad luck. It is still a fault because you were not 'under control'.

Liz Taylor-Webb playing a side-style shot at Bowdon.

What happens if a ball moves between strokes or is accidentially moved between strokes?

It is replaced.

Is there any redress if my opponent misplaces a clip and as a result I take a shot under a misapprehension about the state of the game?

You are entitled to a replay if you realize what has happened before the second stroke of your opponent's next turn.

Can my opponent object if I follow him around the court while he plays a break?

Yes. You should keep off the court altogether during his turn. This rule is usually waived in 'friendly' garden croquet but is enforced at all croquet clubs.

Can I use a marker to help me play a ball to a particular spot?

No. The only marker you can use is your mallet. In doubles, your partner can indicate a spot while you take aim but must move away before you play the stroke.

How do you test whether a ball is wired from another?

A ball is said to be wired from another ball if the path of any part of the first ball to any part of the target ball is impeded by a hoop or the peg, or if a hoop or the peg prevents a free swing of the mallet. The test for normal wiring is shown in Fig. 27. The referee checks that it is the start of the striker's turn and that his opponent is responsible for the position of the ball for which the claim is made. He then places an assistant ball (a spare ball) on the wired side of the object ball in contact with it and another in contact with the hoop

FIG. 27 *Judging whether a ball is wired from another.*

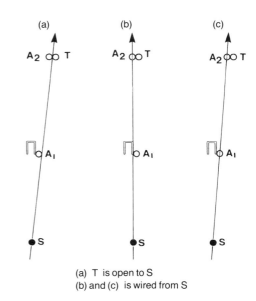

(a) T is open to S
(b) and (c) is wired from S

or peg that is claimed to impede the path of the striker's ball. The referee then inspects the line joining the striker's ball and the two assistant balls. If it is straight or bends towards the object ball, the striker's ball is wired from the object ball.

Are these all the Laws?

No, not all, but they are really all the beginner needs. A booklet containing the Laws of Association Croquet is available from the Croquet Association (address on page 76).

TECHNIQUE

Technique in croquet is divided into two major areas, namely execution and tactics. Execution covers the way strokes are produced. Tactics determine when particular strokes should be played; the tactics of break-play have already been described in 'The Game – A Guide'.

EXECUTION

Execution covers three separate subjects, namely style, grip and stroke play.

Style of play

There are two principal styles of play in use today. Centre style involves swinging the mallet between your legs and is by far the more popular method (Fig. 29). Side style, the standard method of eighty years ago, is still favoured by some tournament players and should not be dismissed out of hand. In practice, most people adopt a form of centre style when they pick up a mallet for the first time and it is distinctly curious that until a group of young Irishmen appeared on the tournament scene in the early 1900s, no-one appeared to have thought of swinging the mallet between the legs rather than to the

FIG. 28

Side style

FIG. 29

Centre style

These comments summarize the main features of each style. Side style involves a more upright stance, permits more powerful shots for less physical effort and is generally less tiring. For these reasons, older players and those whose backs do not take kindly to being bent almost double all day long may prefer it. The only drawback is that side style is a less accurate style for most people because the body is not placed symmetrically over the line of the swing.

Centre style has the advantage of greater accuracy and, provided you can supply the necessary power and are not troubled by a weak back, is the natural choice of most people. It does not matter whether your feet are level or if one is advanced in front of the other. For right-handers it is normal to advance the left foot a little way to improve stability in the swing and vice-versa for left-handers.

Grip

There are three principal methods of gripping the mallet, namely Standard, Irish and Solomon. The Standard Grip is the most usual and the most common grip assumed by beginners above the age of 12 (the reason for this rather gnomic comment will become clear later). For a right-hander, the left hand is placed at the top of the shaft with the knuckles facing forward and the right hand is placed below it with the palm facing forward (Fig. 32). For a left-hander the converse applies.

side. Perhaps the reason was that ladies' costumes effectively forced them to play side style (or even the now discredited golf style) and the gentlemen felt obliged to play the same way. However, the only point of importance is that you should do what seems comfortable and natural.

It is quite common for players who adopt centre style for single ball strokes such as shooting and hoop running and for croquet strokes of moderate strength to switch to a form of side style when they play very heavy roll strokes. Sending two 1lb (454g) balls more than 20yd (18m) on a slow court takes a fair amount of power and the longer backswing available in side style may be essential. It is also quite common to see some side-style players switching to centre style for hoop strokes because they feel it is slightly more accurate.

TECHNIQUE

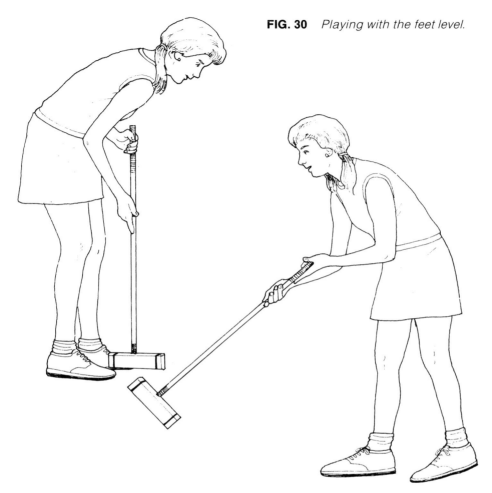

FIG. 30 *Playing with the feet level.*

FIG. 31

Playing with one foot advanced.

The Irish Grip is popular among many tournament players. It owes its name to its use by the young Irishmen referred to earlier who electrified the tournament croquet scene before the First World War with their brilliant shooting and aggressive tactics. For a right-hander, the left hand is again placed at the top of the shaft with the right hand below it but the palms of both hands face forward (Fig. 33). A left-hander simply swaps the hands round. This is not a grip naturally adopted by many beginners and can take some getting used to as it imposes, at least initially, a strain on the wrist of the upper hand. However, its protagonists (who include the author) testify to its great accuracy for single ball strokes of all sorts and, if you are sufficiently muscular, almost any other shot in the book.

The Solomon Grip is named after John Solomon, already mentioned as arguably the greatest player to date. For a right-hander,

FIG. 32

The standard grip

the left hand is again placed at the top of the shaft with the right hand below it but this time the knuckles of both hands face forward (Fig. 34). A left-hander simply swaps the hands around. Solomon adopted this grip as a small boy because it was the only way he could hold a mallet that was taller than himself and the same is true of most young children. It is an interesting grip and can be phenomenally accurate in long shooting as the hands seem to be easy to forget about in the swing and do not tend to fight each other. The Solomon Grip has a reasonable following among tournament players although it is doubtful whether, in the hands of most mortals, it is quite so good for the most precise shots in the game. However, anyone who has seen the play of the elegant New Zealander, Paul Skinley, will have seen perhaps the most accurate croquet ever played with any grip (see page 30).

Stroke play

Stroke play is divided into the following sections:

1 ***Single-ball strokes***
    (a) the plain hit;
    (b) the roquet;
    (c) the rush;
    (d) the hoop stroke.

2 ***Croquet strokes***
    (a) straight croquet strokes;
    (b) split croquet strokes;
    (c) cannons.

FIG. 33

The Irish grip

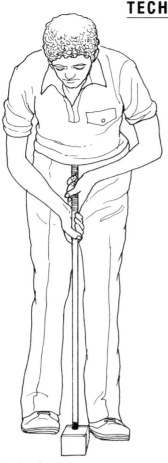

FIG. 34

*The
Solomon grip*

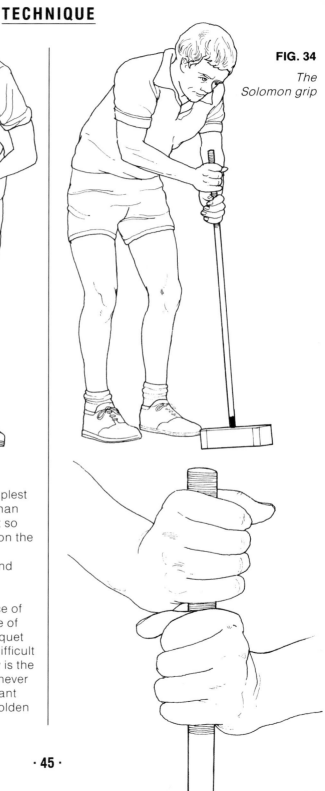

1   Single-ball strokes

(a) The plain hit   A plain hit is the simplest stroke of all. It involves nothing more than striking the striker's ball with the mallet so that the ball goes to the desired point on the court. The opening phase of a game involves plain hits when the players send balls to the boundaries without (intentionally!) hitting another ball.

Do not underestimate the importance of learning how to hit a ball properly. One of the finest coaches in the history of croquet maintained that it was the only really difficult part of the game. Succeed and the sky is the limit. If you frequently miscue, you will never be very successful no matter how brilliant your tactics are! There are just three golden rules:

1. Take aim by taking a few paces back from the striker's ball so that you can walk up to it with your eyes glued to the target. This is called 'stalking' and ensures that your shoulders are square to the line of aim. You will not be consistently accurate merely by standing behind the striker's ball facing the target and twiddling the mallet-head into what looks like the right direction.

2. Take a comfortable stance in which you can keep body movement to an absolute minimum during the swing. If you do this, other maxims involving keeping the head still and the eyes glued to the back of the striker's ball will be obeyed automatically. The distance you stand back from the ball will depend on how upright your style is. The ideal is to ensure that your eyes fall naturally over the back of the ball so that the mallet-head is horizontal at impact with the ball. For most people, the toe of the leading foot will be 9–15in (23–38cm) behind the ball.

3. Take a slow backswing and accelerate the forward swing smoothly into the back of the ball. There should be no jerkiness in the swing and no quitting on impact. Released power should be the essence of the swing.

Practise hitting a ball to specific spots at varying distances. Learn to develop 'touch' so that you can confidently take position in front of a hoop several yards away.

(b) The roquet A roquet is simply a plain hit in which the striker's ball hits one of the other balls on the court. Taking aim properly is obviously crucial and you should focus all your attention on the ball you wish to roquet as you walk up to the striker's ball. Many top players use mental rehearsal to improve their shooting and will make themselves 'see' the striker's ball streaking towards its target in their mind's eye before beginning the swing.

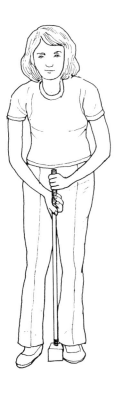

FIG. 35 *Stalking the ball*

Another technique very popular among some younger players is that of 'casting' over the striker's ball before swinging with intent to strike. In effect, the player takes his stance and then rehearses his swing over the ball up to six or eight times before simply extending the backswing and coming in to the ball.

The other rules of plain hitting, namely minimum body movement and a smooth swing, are also very important. The excitement of having a real target leads many beginners to look up to see how the shot has gone and, if they do this too soon, the jerk affects the accuracy of the swing and the direction of the mallet-face. An error of only 1 degree is sufficient to cause you to miss a 10yd (9m) roquet. Some players avoid this by looking at the target ball throughout the swing, in the manner of a snooker or billiards player. It is very successful in the right hands but beginners are unlikely to have a sufficiently grooved swing to make it worthwhile.

If you find your shooting suddenly deteriorating, it is very likely that the amount of body movement has increased. Concentrate on staying steady on your feet throughout the stroke and you will probably notice an immediate improvement.

(c) The rush A rush is simply a roquet in which the roqueted ball is sent to a particular spot. If you are attempting to hit a ball 20yd (18m) away, you will be very pleased to make contact and the ultimate destination of the roqueted ball is not of immediate importance. If the ball to be roqueted is only 12in (30cm) from the striker's ball before the roquet is played, it should be possible to send it somewhere useful in the roquet stroke (Fig. 36).

A long rush is one where the striker's ball is some distance from the object ball before the stroke is played, not to the distance it is hoped to send the rushed ball. For most people, a shot of 3yd (3m) or more is definitely a roquet and not a rush. The

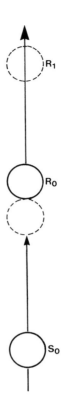

FIG. 36 *A straight rush*

distance between the balls has a significant effect on the amount of power required by the shot. As croquet balls are only imperfectly elastic, greater power is needed to rush a ball 20yd (18m) than to send the striker's ball the same distance in a plain hit.

In addition, the striker's ball leaves the mallet-face with a skidding motion and friction with the ground gradually converts this into rolling motion. If the striker's ball hits the object ball when fully rolling, it will require up to 40% more power to send the object ball a given distance than if the striker's ball hits the object ball while skidding. The distance this conversion occurs in varies with the strength of the shot and the condition of the ground and is soon learned with experience. Well-drained grass just after rain can provide a surface with very little friction on which rushes go like bullets!

You can also attempt to hit the roqueted ball off-centre to send it in a desired direction. This is known as a cut-rush and is governed by the same principles of geometry that apply to snooker and billiards. The larger the degree of cut, the greater the strength of shot required to compensate for the fact that only a fraction of the energy of the striker's ball will be transmitted to the roqueted ball and the greater the risk of missing the ball altogether. Cut-rushes of over 3ft (90cm) are to be avoided.

Good rushing requires particular emphasis on minimizing body movement and maintaining a smooth swing. Beginners often find that the striker's ball jumps when it hits the roqueted ball in a rush and, in extreme cases, can just nick the top of the roqueted ball. This has the embarrassing result that the striker's ball goes much further than the roqueted ball! The answer is to keep still and swing smoothly. If that still does not work, see whether you are standing correctly relative to the striker's ball. Standing either too close or too far away will make it difficult to keep the mallet-head horizontal at impact.

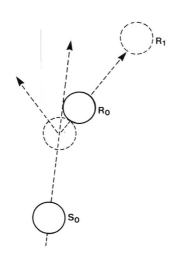

FIG. 37 *A cut-rush*

FIG. 38 *Aiming for a straight hoop stroke.*

(d) The hoop stroke The hoop stroke is simply a roquet in miniature with the difference that you are aiming at a space rather than a ball. At first sight the task seems rather difficult. A ball ($3\frac{5}{8}$in/9cm in diameter) passing cleanly through a tournament hoop ($3\frac{3}{4}$in/9.2cm gap) will leave only $\frac{1}{16}$in (1.5mm) clearance on each side. Indeed, in the President's Cup, the clearance is reduced to $\frac{1}{32}$in on each side.

However, it is easier to run a hoop than you might think for two reasons. First, hoops are mounted in grass and grass in normal British weather has sufficient 'give' to allow even a firmly-set hoop to move slightly when struck by a croquet ball. This gives the hoop a larger effective gap and so allows more margin for error. Second, providing the ball is rolling rather than skidding when it hits an upright, it will often spin through after having been initially checked by an upright. The gentler the stroke, the sooner the striker's ball will start to roll and this is why the hoop stroke should in general be played softly.

All the rules about plain hits apply to hoop-running. Keeping the body still and the swing slow and smooth are reasonably easy given the lack of force required. Aiming requires a little care. If you are absolutely straight in front of the hoop, you can stalk the shot in the normal way using the middle of the gap as your aiming point (Fig. 38).

However, if the shot is at all angled this method will not work because the striker's ball will hit the near upright and bounce across the face of the hoop. The correct way to line up for an angled hoop is to find the line joining the inside edge of the near upright and the side of the ball (Fig. 39). Then stalk the shot by walking up on this line. When you reach the ball, it is very easy to transfer across by a couple of inches so that the mallet-face is squarely behind the middle of the ball. If your swing is accurate, the striker's ball will just miss the near upright and bounce smartly through off the inside of the far upright. It is really surprising from what angles hoops can be run successfully. Depending on the nature of the ground, angles of up to 35 or even 40 degrees can be achieved.

Some players advocate standing closer to the ball than usual to hit slightly down on the ball. This makes the striker's ball start rolling more quickly. However, a ball struck

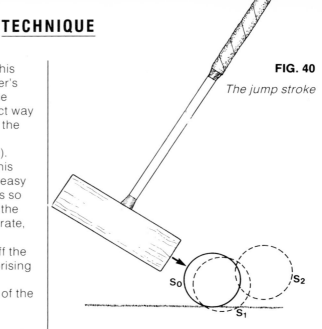

FIG. 40

The jump stroke

S_0 S_1 S_2

accurately in the usual way will acquire quite enough spin to run the hoop. A beginner is advised to concentrate on hitting his ball accurately and normally; what he might gain in extra spin will probably be more than offset by inaccuracy.

Sometimes a hoop will be run if the ball is hit hard against an upright, rebounds by a few inches and then spins through. A form of challenge to an improving player is to see how often he can run hoop 1 from corner 1, a 45-degree angle. Successful attempts usually occur when the ball hits the far upright almost full-on and then spins forward.

The other method of negotiating very angled hoops is to use a jump stroke (Fig. 40). This stroke is played by hitting down on the ball so that its motion has both a vertical and a horizontal component. The grass is compressed and then recovers, forcing the striker's ball into the air. The effect is that the ball acquires added forward spin and, if played well, will just miss the near upright, hit the far upright fairly full a few inches up and then drop to the ground and spin out. The shot works because the ball's aerial flight gives it more time to 'climb' round the far upright.

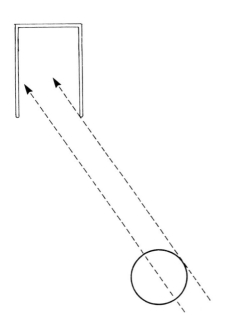

FIG. 39 *Aiming for an angled hoop stroke.*

2 Croquet strokes

A croquet stroke is the first of the two bonus shots earned after making a roquet. The striker's ball is picked up from wherever it came to rest after the roquet and then placed in contact with the roqueted ball in any position the striker chooses. The striker then plays the croquet stroke by hitting the striker's ball so that both balls move or at least shake. Within certain limits, he can vary the direction and the distance travelled of both balls and it is this which gives break-play its tactical potential.

(a) Straight croquet strokes Straight croquet strokes are played by striking the striker's ball in the same direction as the line of centres of the balls. The distance that the croqueted ball can be sent relative to the striker's ball can be varied from 10:1 to 1:2. The variation is achieved by modifications to the stance, the grip and the way the ball is hit. Although the variation of the distance ratio is a continuous process, it is conventional to identify five different straight croquet strokes. These are the stop-shot (7–10:1), drive (3–4:1), half roll (2:1), full roll (1:1) and pass roll (1:2).

Although the list given above is in order of decreasing distance ratio, the starting point is the drive because this is the basic shot from which the others are developed.

FIG. 41 *The drive*

1 **The drive** This is played exactly the same way as a plain hit with your normal stance and grip and with a normal amount of follow-through. There is no effort to check the mallet or to stress the follow-through. Although the distance ratio obtained will depend on the weight of the mallet, the nature of the ground and your own style, it should be in the region of 3–4:1. If it is well outside this range, something is wrong.

2 **The half roll** Stand nearer the balls so that your leading foot is only an inch or two behind the level of the striker's ball. Do not alter the width of your stance. Grip the mallet 3–4in (8–10cm) lower down, particularly with the lower hand. The combination of these stance and grip changes will automatically cause you to crouch a little and raise the back of the mallet slightly. The stroke is played firmly to hit the striker's ball a little above centre and with moderate emphasis on the follow-through. The striker's ball should travel half as far as the croqueted ball.

FIG. 42 *The half roll*

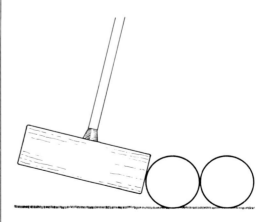

John Solomon playing with the Solomon grip.

FIG. 43 *The full roll*

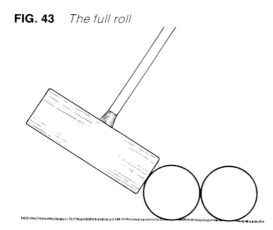

FIG. 44 *The pass roll*

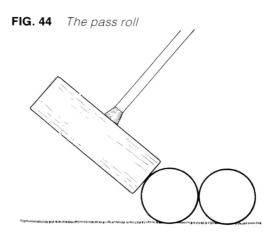

3 The full roll Stand still nearer the balls so that your leading foot is level with or an inch or two in front of the striker's ball. Grip the mallet halfway down with the upper hand and just above the head with the lower hand. The combination of these stance and grip changes will automatically cause you to adopt a distinctly crouched position and to raise the back of the mallet and tilt the shaft forwards. The stroke is played firmly to hit down at 10 to 10.30 on the clock-face with pronounced follow-through. The striker's ball should travel as far as the croqueted ball. Many centre-style players play full rolls with a side style.

4 The pass roll The pass roll requires the same approach as the full roll but carried to slightly greater extremes. It is not a shot that a beginner can expect to play immediately as it is very easy to commit a fault such as a push. The secret is to take a slow backswing and accelerate the mallet head smoothly and very firmly through the balls so that the striker's ball remains in contact with the mallet and the croqueted ball for long enough to acquire extra forward spin. In a well-played pass roll, the striker's ball will travel just behind the croqueted ball for the first few yards and then accelerate past it as the spin takes effect.

5 The stop-shot Stand about 6in (15cm) further back from the balls than you would for a drive and grip the mallet at the very top of the shaft. The combination of these stance and grip changes will automatically cause you to raise the front of the mallet and tilt the shaft backwards. The stroke is played firmly to hit up on the striker's ball at 8.30 on the clock-face with no follow-through. Some players attempt to ground the mallet at the same time as it hits the ball to minimize follow-through but this is not essential. The croqueted ball should travel at least six times as far as the striker's ball.

The stop-shot requires assiduous practice because it does take a certain knack to play it well and because it should be the basis of all hoop approaches and all really good break-play. This is because it is the croquet stroke in which the striker's ball moves least in relation to the croqueted ball and thus has the least absolute error potential. Consider sending a pioneer into position 25yd (23m) away in a stroke in which the striker's ball approaches the pilot ball at the next hoop. If the stroke is played as a full roll, a 20% error in strength will send the striker's ball 5 yd (5m) too far or too short, a very missable distance from the pilot. If the croquet stroke had been a 10:1 ratio stop-shot, the same error would result in an absolute error in the position of the striker's ball of only 18in (45cm).

(b) Split croquet strokes The croqueted ball will always move in the direction of the line of centres but the striker can vary the direction in which the striker's ball moves, the line of departure, by swinging the mallet at an angle to the line of centres. This angle is referred to as the angle of swing. The line of departure is also affected by the type of stroke played and by the phenomenon known as 'pull'.

1 General It used to be thought that the line of swing could be determined by bisecting the angle between the line of centres and the line of departure. This works reasonably well for shots where the angle of swing is less than 45 degrees and the striker's ball and the croqueted ball have to travel similar distances. It does not work well in other cases and it is far better to plot mentally the positions on the court you wish the two balls to occupy after the stroke and to determine the spot halfway between the destinations (Fig. 47). That is the point which will give a reliable line of swing subject to the type of shot you wish to play.

FIG. 45   *The stop-shot*

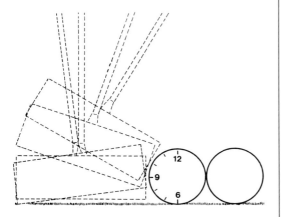

FIG. 46

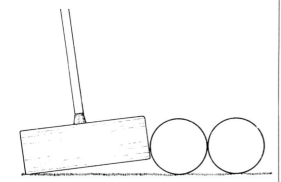

The clock-face guide to various croquet strokes.

FIG. 47

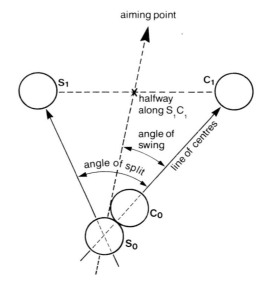

. *Finding the aiming point in a split croquet stroke.*

FIG. 48 (a)

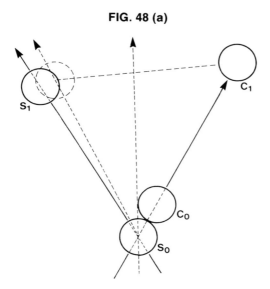

Roll-stroke effect – narrowing the angle of split.

FIG. 48 (b)

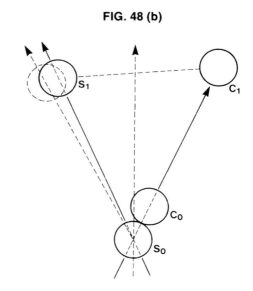

Stop-shot effect – widening the angle of split.

In a roll stroke the striker's ball is held in contact with the croqueted ball and so tends to follow the line of swing more closely than you might otherwise expect. In a stop-shot, the reverse applies and a wider angle of divergence can be achieved (Figs. 48 a&b).

It is not possible to achieve an angle of divergence of more than 90 degrees. If the angle of swing is increased beyond 45 degrees the angle of departure remains at 90 degrees but less of the energy of the stroke is transmitted to the croqueted ball (Figs. 49 a&b). In the extreme case, when the angle of swing is 90 degrees, the croqueted ball only shakes and virtually all the energy goes into the striker's ball. This is the croquet stroke known as a take-off which is described below.

It cannot be stressed too much that croquet strokes have to be practised intensively. Good players do not calculate when they play them, instead they look at the places the balls must go to and rely on muscle memory to hit the striker's ball in the right direction, in the right place and with the right strength to achieve the desired outcome. It is quite easy to learn but it does take a little time to acquire the necessary experience.

2 **The take-off** The take-off is an important stroke, particularly for beginners, because it is used extensively to send the striker's ball across the lawn to get within range of the enemy balls. It is the croquet stroke nearest a single-ball stroke in character and the development of sufficient touch to be able to take-off accurately over 35–40yd (32–37m) is an important step in a novice's career.

When setting the balls for a take-off it is important to gauge the right-angle correctly. Two methods can be recommended. In the first, the mallet is used as a T-square and the head is placed in contact with the balls so that the shaft indicates the line of departure (Fig. 50a). The other method, to which players tend to graduate as experience grows, is to

FIG. 49 (a)

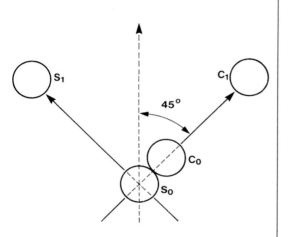

45° angle of swing, 90° angle of split, $S_0 S_1 = C_0 C_1$.

FIG. 49 (b)

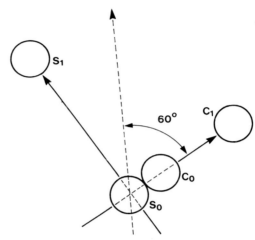

66° angle of swing, 90° angle of split, $S_0 S_1$ is greater than $C_0 C_1$.

identify the 'arrow-heads' formed by the spaces between the surfaces of the balls and to use the notional arrow shafts to indicate the line (Fig. 50b).

As the croqueted ball must at least shake when the croquet stroke is played, it is important to play slightly into the croqueted ball. In practice, take-offs should be played only after checking carefully (i) that the balls are actually in contact, and (ii) are not liable to roll slightly apart while the swing is in progress. The angle of swing should be 85–88 degrees (Fig. 51a). This ensures that a modicum of energy is transmitted to the croqueted ball. Committing a fault by failing to shake the croqueted ball is one of the commoner mistakes by beginners.

The thick take-off is simply a take-off in which the angle of swing is decreased to 70–80 degrees. It is often useful to move the croqueted ball a few feet or yards while sending the striker's ball to another ball (Fig. 51b). When the angle

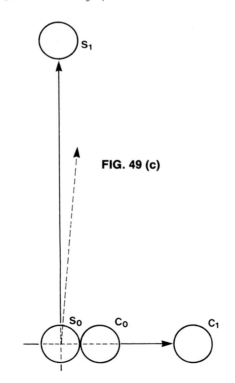

FIG. 49 (c)

CROQUET

FIG. 50 (a)

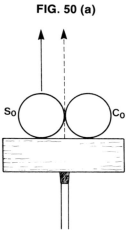

Using the mallet shaft.

FIG. 50 (b)

So   Co

Using the arrow-head.

FIG. 51 (a)

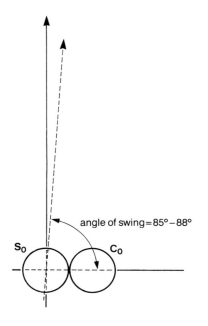

angle of swing=85°–88°

Thin take-off

FIG. 51 (b)

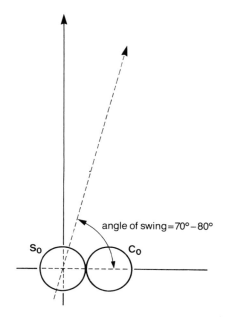

angle of swing=70°–80°

Thick take-off

TECHNIQUE

swing is reduced to 50–60 degrees the stroke could be equally well described as a split pass roll.

3 The hoop approach Hoop approaches are the croquet strokes which require the most accuracy. If you make a mess of a croquet stroke when approaching another ball, you may be able to survive by hitting the roquet. If you mis-approach a hoop, you are dead. There are three golden rules:

(a) You should always play to obtain a forward rush after running the hoop. This means that in the hoop approach the pilot must be sent to a point on the non-playing side of the hoop where it is easy to get the rush you want. It is generally less taxing on the nerves to run a hoop with a modicum of firmness than at dead weight, so send the pilot well forward (Figs. 52 a&b).

(b) The above requirement makes a stop-shot the first choice for the hoop approach in all cases where you are approaching from reasonably close by. A stop-shot should also be your second and third choice as well! In short, only play a drive or, worse still, a roll if you cannot avoid it. The other reason for preferring stop-shots is the much lower absolute error already discussed in section 2(a) (5) above.

(c) If you are approaching from the side, you will realize that over-hitting and under-hitting by the same amount may not have the same effect. If the striker's ball will move towards the hoop in the approach, an under-hit is less immediately fatal than an over-hit and the destination for the striker's ball should be biased slightly in favour of under-hitting (Fig. 53). If the striker's ball will move away from the

hoop, an over-hit will be safer and the destination for the striker's ball should be biased that way (Fig. 54).

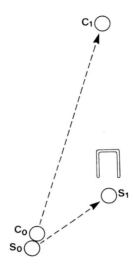

FIG. 52 (a)

A good approach to hoop 1, ball C_1 is well forward.

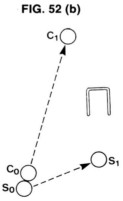

FIG. 52 (b)

A poor approach to hoop 1, ball C_1 is too close to the hoop.

FIG. 53

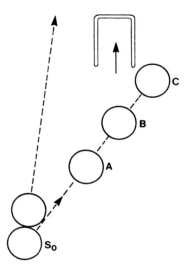

Approaching from the playing side – the hoop can be run from positions A and B but not from C.

FIG. 54

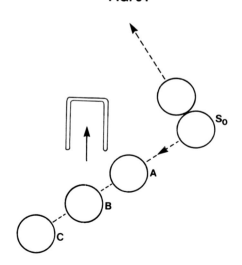

Approaching from the non-playing side – the hoop can be run from positions B and C, but not from A.

TACTICS

Level play

If you have the innings, your tactics should be based on attempting to win the game as quickly as possible without taking unnecessary risks. If your opponent has the innings, you must be vigilant for every opportunity to take the innings from him by hitting a safe long roquet but, if no safe shot is available, you must play to impede his progress as much as possible in the hope that he will either get bogged down or overreach himself and break down.

Using the innings You have the innings if you can begin your next turn with a short roquet and you take the innings from your opponent if he leaves you a long shot which you hit. In each case the ideal is to create a 4-ball break as soon as possible and then conduct it to a successful conclusion, namely a good leave or, possibly, victory itself. The reason for emphasizing a 4-ball break as the objective is because this is the easiest break to play. We looked at such a break in 'The Game – A Guide' but you cannot assume that the pick-up will always be as straightforward as it was for Andrew in that example.

In fact, when you begin a turn with the innings you should immediately decide which of the following situations applies:
1   A 3- or 4-ball break exists which will probably give your opponent the innings if you make a mistake.
2   A break is possible but you can get a good leave and retain the innings if you do not make progress.
3   There is no realistic chance of a break and you should concentrate on getting a good leave.

1   *The immediate break* It almost always pays to go for the break if possible. Attacking croquet is enjoyable croquet and you will improve much more quickly than if

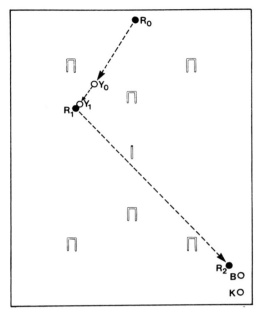

FIG. 55 (a)   *Stroke 1 – Red hits Yellow. Stroke 2 – croquet stroke (take-off) sending Red close to Blue.*

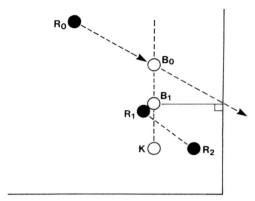

FIG. 55 (b)

Stroke 3 – Red roquets Blue sending it over the boundary, Blue is replaced on the yard-line at B_1. Stroke 4 – Red takes off to R_2 to obtain a rush on Black.

you concentrate on not taking risks. There will normally be a good chance of a 3-ball break at least if you start a turn with at least one enemy ball out in the court and a rush somewhere constructive, namely your next hoop or towards the open ball, or if you hit in with the enemy balls joined up.

Fig. 55(a) shows a typical position after you have hit in with red on yellow with blue and black joined up in corner 4. Red wants hoop 1, yellow has finished up near hoop 6 and the chance is there. At least as important, it is not very easy to send yellow to the safety of a boundary and get close enough to the enemy to separate them. So you might as well go for the break anyway. Take-off from yellow to the enemy, hit one (blue) and take-off to get a good rush on black to hoop 1. Make sure you aim the rush at least 2yd (2m) to the playing side (south) of the hoop so that you can play a stop-shot approach which will place black well to the

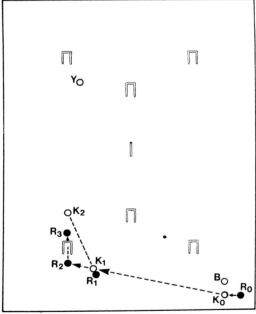

FIG. 55 (c)   *Stroke 5 – Red rushes Black to hoop 1. Stroke 6 – croquet stroke (hoop approach) sending Black beyond the hoop and Red into position to run. Stroke 7 – Red runs hoop 1.*

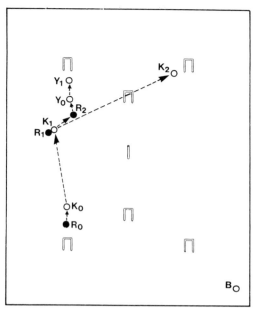

FIG. 56 (a)   *Stroke 8 – Red rushes Black towards Yellow.*
Stroke 9 – croquet stroke sending Black to hoop 3 and Red close to Yellow.
Stroke 10 – Red roquets Yellow close to hoop 2.

north (Fig. 55b). Run hoop 1, rush black just short of yellow, stop-shot black to within 3ft (90cm) of hoop 3 and get a good rush on yellow to hoop 2 (Fig. 55c). Make hoop 2 with a rush on yellow to a spot 4yd (4m) north of black, play the rush and stop-shot yellow down to hoop 4 (preferably 2–3ft (60–90cm) south-east for reasons which will soon be clear) and make hoop 3 off black with a forward rush (Figs. 55 a,b&c).

What about blue in corner 4, you may ask. This is where an important principle should be stated. When you need to extract a ball from a corner to develop a 3-ball break into a 4-ball break, you should normally wait until just before you run the adjacent hoop.

Hence, in this case, you rush black after making hoop 3 south of hoop 4, take-off to blue in corner 4, roquet it and in the croquet stroke split blue to hoop 5 as a pioneer while

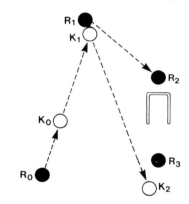

▲ **FIG. 56 (c)**   *Stroke 15 – Red roquets Black north of hoop 3.*
Stroke 16 – croquet stroke (hoop approach) sending Black beyond the hoop and Red into position to run.
Stroke 17 – Red runs hoop 3.

◀ **FIG. 56 (b)**   *Stroke 11 – croquet stroke (hoop approach) sending Yellow beyond the hoop and Red into position to run.*
Stroke 12 – Red runs hoop 2.
Stroke 13 – Red rushes Yellow north of hoop 3.
Stroke 14 – croquet stroke sending Yellow south-east of hoop 4 and Red close to Black.

**David Openshaw using the standard grip to play a half
jump shot over another ball blocking the hoop.**

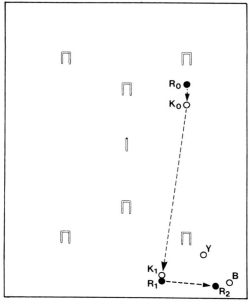

FIG. 57 (a)

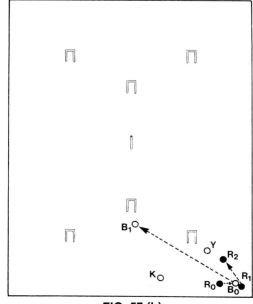

FIG. 57 (b)

red comes to rest with a rush on yellow to hoop 4 (Figs. 57 a&b). The fact that yellow was between the hoop and the corner made the split much easier. This is a good example of the use of foresight in croquet tactics. If you had not needed to extract blue from the corner, the correct place for yellow would have been 3ft (90cm) to the north or north-west of hoop 4.

You complete the development of a 4-ball break by approaching hoop 4 off yellow, with yellow kept close to the hoop, running hoop 4 hard to the boundary and then roqueting black, waiting conveniently close by. Now black can be croqueted to hoop 6 while red goes to yellow, yellow can be rushed closer to blue at hoop 5 and croqueted to the vicinity of the peg and you have a perfect 4-ball break (Figs. 57c, 58a&b).

The last point to make concerns what to do when things go wrong in the course of a break. If a bad approach leaves a nasty hoop, ask yourself what you give away if you

miss. Never risk giving your opponent an easy break unless you are 75% sure you will be successful or there is simply no safe option available. In Fig. 59 you have over-rolled hoop 5 off the enemy blue and left yourself a very angled hoop shot. Black is at hoop 6 and partner, yellow, is in corner 4. Unless you are playing an expert, the correct move is to rejoin partner and hope that blue misses black.

If yellow was instead a pivot ball near the peg and thus within a few yards of both blue and black, joining partner would be madness and you might well feel that little more would be lost by trying the hoop. Although positive croquet is good croquet, mad croquet is bad croquet and your praiseworthy urge to make progress at all costs should be capable of moderation when the circumstances demand it.

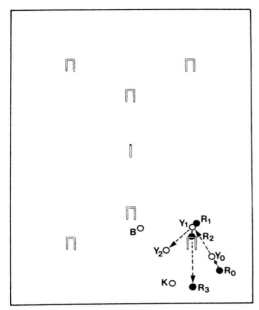

FIG. 57 (c)

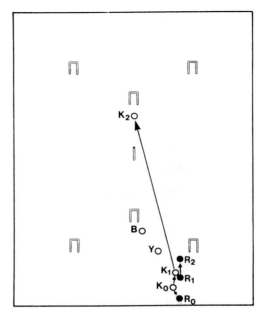

FIG. 58 (a)

FIG. 57 (a)

*Stroke 18 – Red rushes Black to the south
boundary.*
*Stroke 19 – croquet stroke in which Red
takes off close to Blue.*

FIG. 57 (b)

Stroke 20 – Red roquets Blue.
*Stroke 21 – croquet stroke sending Blue to
hoop 5 and Red close to yellow.*

FIG. 57 (c)

*Stroke 22 – Red roquets Yellow north of
hoop 4.*
*Stroke 23 – croquet stroke (hoop approach)
in which Yellow is sent to Y_2 and Red takes
position to run.*
Stroke 24 – Red runs hoop 4.

FIG. 58 (a)

Stroke 25 – Red roquets Black.
*Stroke 26 – croquet stroke sending Black to
hoop 6 and Red close to Yellow.*

FIG. 58 (b)

Stroke 27 – Red roquets Yellow.
*Stroke 28 – croquet stroke sending Yellow
near the peg and Red close to Blue.*

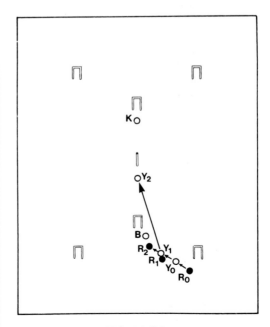

FIG. 58 (b)

CROQUET

FIG. 59

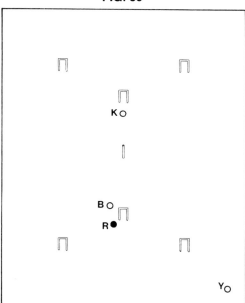

FIG. 60 (a)

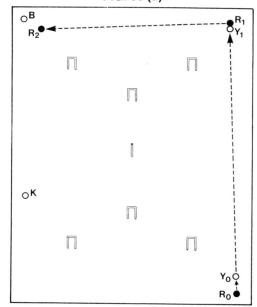

2 Hedging your bets In (Fig. 60a) you
have the classic position after the enemy has
missed his own tice in turn 4. You play red
and rush yellow near corner 3, take-off to
blue in corner 2, roquet it and take-off down
the west yard-line to black (Fig. 60b). If it is
your lucky day the take-off leaves red close
enough to black to rush black to hoop 1
(Fig. 60c). A good hoop approach and a
controlled hoop will give you a rush towards
yellow waiting in corner 3 and the chance of
an immediate break (Fig. 60d).

Often you will be unable to get away
immediately and will have to leave black
near (but not in front of) hoop 1 and end
the turn by sending red back to yellow to
leave a rush out of corner 3 towards either
blue or hoop 1 (Fig. 61). You have made
little progress but have established a
superior position that will probably
force your opponent to defend by sending
black into corner 4 while you will still
have a chance of establishing a 3-ball break
which can then be developed into a 4-ball
break.

FIG. 60 (b)

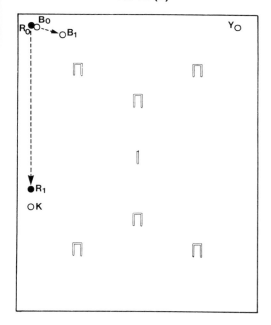

FIG. 60 (c)

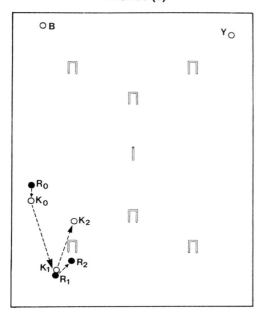

FIG. 60 (d)

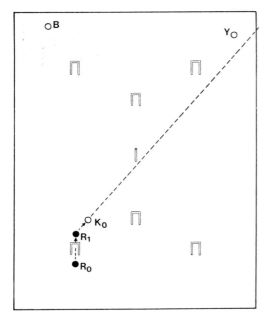

FIG. 59
Red has over-approached hoop 5.

FIG. 60 (a)
Stroke 1 – Red rushes Yellow to the north boundary.
Stroke 2 – croquet stroke in which Red takes off close to Blue.

FIG. 60 (b)
Stroke 3 – Red roquets Blue.
Stroke 4 – croquet stroke in which Red takes off close to Black.

FIG. 60 (c)
Stroke 5 – Red rushes Black south of hoop 1.
Stroke 6 – croquet stroke (hoop approach) sending Black beyond hoop 1 and Red into position to run.

FIG. 60 (d)
Stroke 7 – Red runs hoop 1.
Stroke 8 – Red rushes Black up to Yellow.

FIG. 61
A useful leave.

FIG. 61

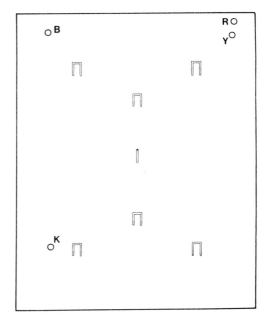

CROQUET

3 Guaranteeing the leave Sometimes you cannot have your cake and eat it too. In (Fig. 62) your opponent has shown great respect for your formidable reputation and has joined up 20yd (18m) apart on the east boundary while you are laid up in corner 2 and want to make hoop 1 with red. You rush yellow 4yd (4m) south-west of hoop 1 and review the position.

Your opponent would love you to try the hoop and make a mess of it so that he can take a free shot with blue at black down the east boundary with a break laid if he hits. For once you decide that discretion is the better part of valour and take-off from yellow to black. You roquet black, split it just to the west of hoop 2 while red goes to blue (Fig. 63). Roquet blue and play a thick take-off so that blue moves 3yd (3m) in-court while red returns to yellow to lay a perfect rush to hoop 1 and no double target for either enemy ball (Fig. 64).

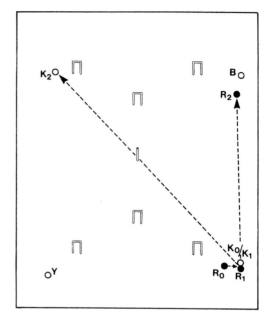

FIG. 63

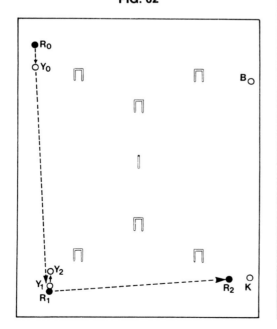

FIG. 62

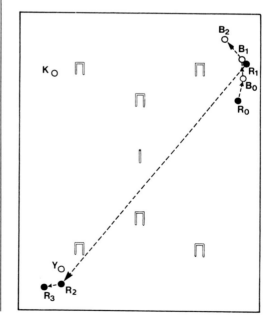

FIG. 64

This is how a good player gets a controlled leave. He ensures that the last two strokes of his turn consist of a croquet stroke, usually a take-off, which returns the striker's ball to its partner followed by a final positional shot from close range. He also avoids leaving the dreaded double target, two balls that seem only a few inches apart from the perspective of his opponent (Fig. 65).

Such a target is hit more often than you might expect because the opponent shoots with more confidence than usual and therefore swings more smoothly and hits a better shot. Many players will take on a 24yd (22m) double more happily than a 12yd (11m) single-ball target for this reason.

Defending The outplayer has a simple choice when he steps onto the court. Should he shoot or should he finesse (play defensively)? If he shoots, with which ball and at which ball? If he finesses, with which ball and where should it go? For the beginner, the advice should be to take every chance to shoot provided that a miss will not hand your opponent a 4-ball break on a plate. You will be playing other beginners and players who are not yet expert and you will only occasionally be punished for over-exuberant play. The choice of which ball to play is simple: always play the ball of more use to your opponent. In (Fig. 66) blue is for hoop 1 and has left red at hoop 2 and yellow near the middle of the east boundary. Red is obviously more useful, being a pioneer for hoop 2, and must be moved.

Finessing means playing a positional shot into a corner or elsewhere on the yard-line to remove a ball from the opponent's break and so make life more difficult for him in the hope that he will break down. A wide join with partner is relatively aggressive because it threatens a possible roquet if you are not disturbed. Sending a ball into a corner is more defensive. Finessing is appropriate in expert play and beginners should defend when necessary but will generally do better to have a go.

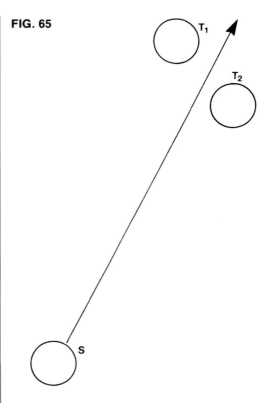

FIG. 65

FIG. 62
Stroke 1 – Red rushes Yellow south of hoop 1.
Stroke 2 – croquet stroke in which Red takes off to Black.

FIG. 63
Stroke 3 – Red roquets Black.
Stroke 4 – croquet stroke sending Black to hoop 2 and Red close to Blue.

FIG. 64
Stroke 5 – Red roquets Blue.
Stroke 6 – croquet stroke (thick take-off) which moves Blue a short distance into court and sends Red back to Yellow.
Stroke 7 – Red takes position to rush Yellow to hoop 1 in the next turn.

FIG. 65
A double target for S – although T_1 and T_2 are more than one diameter apart, S cannot pass between them from where it lies.

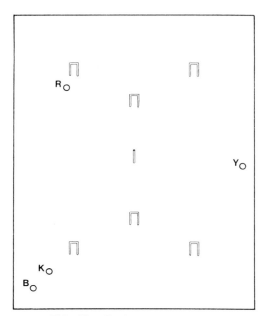

FIG. 66 *Red must be moved.*

Handicap play

Croquet has a well-established handicap system which enables players of all abilities to compete on effectively equal terms. Handicaps range from -2 (expert) to 16 (beginners). In a game played under the laws of handicap play the weaker player or 'higher-bisquer' receives extra turns called bisques equal in number to the difference between the handicaps of the two players. Bisques are graduated in half-bisques from -2 to 8 and thereafter in whole bisques. Thus, if a 12 plays a $-1\frac{1}{2}$, the 12 handicapper receives $13\frac{1}{2}$ bisques.

A bisque is used at the end of the bisque-receiver's previous turn and entitles him to commence a new turn as if he had just stepped onto the court. If the bisque-receiver has several bisques he can use them one after the other if he wishes. A half-bisque is a restricted extra turn in which

The author lining up a peel against the United States team.

the striker can roquet all the other balls but may not score a point. Half-bisques only occur if one of the players' handicaps contains a half.

Traditionally, bisques are indicated by white sticks about 6in (15cm) long which are stuck into the turf by the side of the court and pulled up as they are used. A half-bisque is indicated by a smaller stick. The bisque-receiver is obliged to make a clear indication by word or gesture that he wishes to take a bisque at the end of his current turn and before he leaves the court.

Bisques should be used constructively to create and maintain breaks. When used properly, typically by a senior player whose tactical abilities are unimpaired, they are extremely powerful. When used by beginners, the story is often one of missed opportunities or panic-struck squandering when the innings could be surrendered temporarily and valuable bisques conserved.

The opening   The existence of bisques naturally affects opening tactics. If the bisque-receiver wins the toss, he should choose to play second so that he and not his stronger opponent has the first chance to play with all four balls on court. The tactics of the bisque-giver will depend on the number of bisques given and his own standard of play. If there are only a few bisques to be given or his handicap is higher than 2, a standard opening is appropriate so that the bisque-receiver has to work as hard as possible to get a break.

If the bisque-giver is an expert giving a 'fence' of bisques to an opponent who he suspects of being better than his handicap (often the case with young and rapidly-improving players), bolder tactics are called for. In turn 1, the expert will play a ball to a spot 4–5yd (4–5m) north of hoop 1 and shoot at the enemy ball in turn 3 no matter where it is sent in turn 2. If he hits, he has a good chance of an immediate 3-ball break to take the striker's ball to rover or the peg and thus inflict a vital psychological blow.

Break creation   It is possible for any medium-bisquer (handicap 3 to 7) to establish a 4-ball break using only one bisque no matter where the enemy balls are at the start of the turn. Higher-bisquers, once they have learned the basics of the full range of croquet strokes and can rush with some degree of confidence, should be able to set up such a break using two bisques.

Consider the position in (Fig. 67(a)). Jonathan is a 12-handicapper receiving 8 bisques and starts his turn with blue and black both for hoop 1 and close together near corner 4 (positions B_0 and K_0). His opponent has put the other balls in as unhelpful a position as possible, namely red in corner 2 and yellow near corner 3, in the hope that Jonathan will waste his bisques. This is hardly a promising position but let us see what two effectively-used bisques can do.

FIG. 67 (a)
Stroke 1 – Blue rushes Black near to hoop 5.
Stroke 2 – croquet stroke sending Black towards hoop 1 and Blue towards Red.
Stroke 3 – Blue misses Red and is replaced on the yard-line at B_3.
FIG. 67 (b)
Stroke 4 – Blue roquets Red which is replaced on the corner-spot.
Stroke 5 – croquet stroke (full roll) sending Red and Blue near hoop 3.
Stroke 6 – Blue misses Yellow and is replaced on the yard-line at B_3.
FIG. 67 (c)
Stroke 7 – Blue roquets Yellow.
Stroke 8 – croquet stroke (straight drive) sending Yellow to hoop 2 and Blue close to Red.
FIG. 67 (d)
Stroke 9 – Blue rushes Red towards the peg.
Stroke 10 – croquet stroke (take-off) in which Red barely moves and Blue is sent close to Black.

TECHNIQUE

FIG. 67 (a)

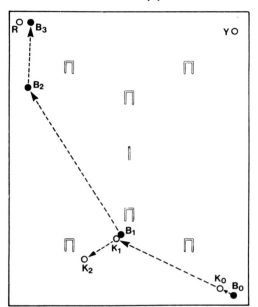

FIG. 67 (c)

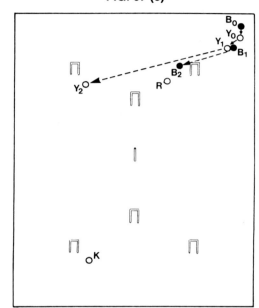

FIG. 67 (b)

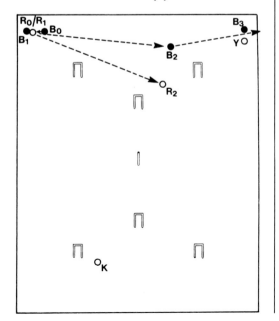

FIG. 67 (d)

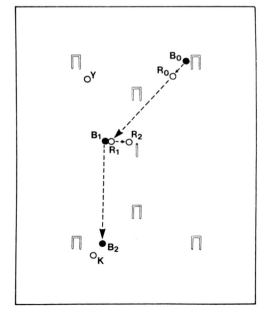

Jonathan chooses to play with blue because it has a rush of sorts towards the middle of the court and he starts the turn by rushing black as far as possible towards hoop 1. In fact, it ends up near hoop 5. In the croquet stroke, he plays a thick take-off in which he concentrates on getting black to stop as close to hoop 1 as possible while blue, the striker's ball, travels towards red in corner 2. However, this is a difficult shot for a fairly inexperienced player and he is not surprised that although black is quite good blue ends up several yards short of target. In the continuation stroke, Jonathan attempts to roquet red but misses, blue being replaced on the yard-line a few inches east of red at B_3 (see Fig. 67(a)).

He now takes a bisque and begins this new turn by making the easy roquet on red. In the croquet stroke, he plays a straight full roll, a stroke which many beginners find quite easy, in which both red and blue are sent towards hoop 3. In the continuation stroke, Jonathan tries to roquet yellow but again misses (Fig. 67(b)). However, the situation is now quite promising.

Jonathan takes a second bisque and roquets yellow. The croquet stroke is a straight drive which sends yellow to hoop 2 and leaves blue a yard or so short of red (Fig. 67(c)). In the continuation stroke, he rushes red as far as possible towards the peg. He now plays the beginner's favourite croquet stroke, the take-off, to leave red where it is and send blue down to black waiting at hoop 1 (Fig. 67(d)).

He has now set up a 4-ball break with a pilot (black), pivot (red) and pioneer (yellow) in the right positions using standard strokes none of which demanded very great accuracy. In practice, Jonathan might easily have saved a bisque by hitting red first time. It is quite commonplace for a bisque-receiver to make use of the same bisque several times over by hitting missable roquets because the presence of the bisque enabled him to take the shot in a relaxed frame of mind.

Coping with mistakes Although handicapping is essentially subjective, an approximate method of estimating an unknown player's true handicap is to ask him to play a 4-ball break from hoop 1 to the peg and count the number of bisques he needs to compensate for errors of execution. His handicap is then set at twice that number as he has two balls to conduct to the peg in a game. Thus, although we left Jonathan with a straightforward 4-ball break in the previous section, he can be expected to use up to 6 bisques in the course of taking blue to the peg. However, the way in which these bisques are used can vary greatly.

Suppose Jonathan maintains the 4-ball break until hoop 3 when he over-approaches and has no possibility of running the hoop. How should he use the last stroke of that turn if he intends to take a bisque to continue the break? In Fig. 68 he has a perfect 4-ball break with the pivot and pioneer in good position. He may be tempted

FIG. 68

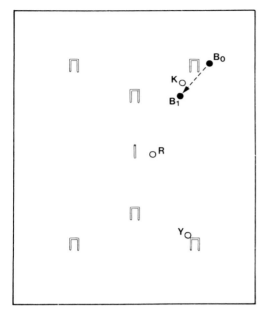

Stroke 1 – Blue is played to leave an easy rush on Black.

to use his last continuation stroke to play blue into hoop-running position so that the bisque is used just to run the hoop. However, this would be a mistake on most occasions. Unless the pilot ball is ideally positioned and the stroke required to place the striker's ball in position for the hoop is really trivial, it is better to use the last stroke to obtain a rush on the pilot and use the bisque to rush the pilot to the playing side of the hoop so that it can be re-approached.

However, on most occasions there is a still better use for the last stroke of the turn and the bisque, Fig. 69(a). This represents an all too common situation where Jonathan had a decidedly imperfect 4-ball break before making his mistake when approaching hoop 3. Now the impending bisque should be used to repair the break, not just to make the next hoop. Jonathan should use the last stroke of his turn to send blue off the south boundary beyond yellow so that it is replaced on the yard-line at B_1. The bisque turn commences by a roquet on yellow which sends it to the playing side of hoop 4 and continues with a take-off to red (Fig. 69(b)) and a roquet which returns it to the area of the peg. A take-off to black at hoop 3 allows Jonathan to re-approach hoop 3 as before but now with a much better break (Fig. 69(c)).

CROQUET

FIG. 69 (a)

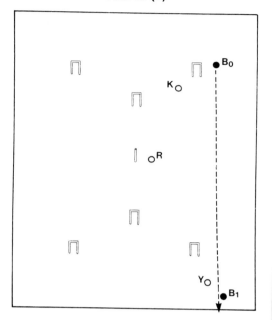

FIG. 69 (b)

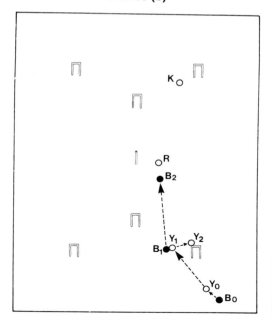

FIG. 69 (c)

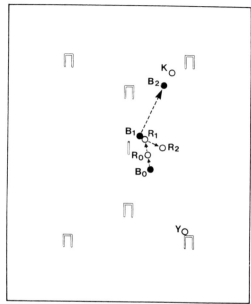

FIG. 69 (a)

Stroke 1 – Blue is sent off the boundary beyond Yellow and a bisque is taken.

FIG. 69 (b)

Stroke 2 – Blue rushes Yellow to hoop 4.
Stroke 3 – croquet stroke (take-off) leaving Yellow at hoop 4 and sending Blue to Red.

FIG. 69 (c)

Stroke 4 – Blue roquets Red gently.
Stroke 5 – croquet stroke (take-off) leaving Red near the peg and sending Blue close to Black.

William Prichard playing side style with the right foot forward.

USEFUL
ADDRESSES

The Croquet Association
The Secretary
The Hurlingham Club
Ranelagh Gardens
London SW6 3PR
01-736-3148

Federation of East Anglian Croquet Clubs
The Secretary
16 Wellpond Close
Sharnbrook
Bedford MK44 1PL
0234-781783

Federation of East Midland Croquet Clubs
The Secretary
9 Fairmount Drive
Loughborough
Leicestershire LE11 3JR
0509-263954

Frederation of Northern Croquet Clubs
The Secretary
9 Langham Road
Bowdon
Altrincham
Cheshire WA14 2HT
061-941-3579

Federation of South East Region Croquet Clubs
The Secretary
35 Shirley Avenue
Old Coulsdon
Surrey CR3 1QY
01-668-6525

Federation of South West Croquet Clubs
The Secretary
36 Old Snead Avenue
Stoke Bishop
Bristol BS9 1SE
0272-682255

USEFUL ADDRESSES

Federation of West Midlands Croquet Clubs
The Secretary
21 The Fold
Penn
Wolverhampton WV4 5QY
0902-336832

Australian Croquet Association
The Secretary
1 Wyvern Street
Epping
New South Wales 2121
Australia

Croquet Canada
The Secretary
159 Walmer Road
Toronto
Canada

Croquet Association of Ireland
The Secretary
20 Aubrey Road
Shankhill
Co. Dublin
Eire

Croquet Association of Japan
President
Isebu, Bld 1F 2-11-20
Amakubo, Sakuramura
Niiharugun, Ibaragi
Japan

New Zealand Croquet Council
The Secretary
21 Egmont Street
Hawera
New Zealand

Scottish Croquet Association
The Chairman
26 Craig Street
Airdrie
Scotland ML6 9AJ

South African Croquet Association
The Secretary
42 Howick Road
Pietermaritzburg
Natal 3201
Republic of South Africa

United States Croquet Association
The Secretary
500 Avenue of Champions
Palm Beach Gardens
Florida 33418
USA

Welsh Croquet Association
The Secretary
60 Coleridge Avenue
Penarth
S. Glamorgan
Wales

RULES CLINIC
INDEX

**Bob Jackson of New Zealand lining up a peel during
the British Open Championships at Hurlingham in 1986.**

INDEX